Happy Cute

Happy Cute

25 Amigurumi Gifts to Celebrate Special Occasions

Annie Obaachan

A QUANTUM BOOK

First edition for the United States, its territories and
possessions, Canada, and the Philippines published
in 2012 by Barron's Educational Series, Inc.

All inquiries should be addressed to:
Barron's Educational Series, Inc.
250 Wireless Boulevard
Hauppauge, New York 11788
www.barronseduc.com

ISBN-13: 978-1-4380-0024-4

Library of Congress Control Number:
2011926018

This book is published and produced by
Quantum Books
6 Blundell Street
London N7 9BH

QUMHC2A

Design: Jeremy Tilston
Photographer: Simon Pask
Managing Editor: Julie Brooke
Project Editor: Samantha Warrington
Assistant Editor: Jo Morley
Production Manager: Rohana Yusof
Publisher: Sarah Bloxham

All images are the copyright of Quantum Publishing.

Printed and bound in Singapore by Star Standard
Industries (Pte) Ltd.

9 8 7 6 5 4 3 2 1

Contents

Cute, Cute, Cute: Welcome to the Wonderful World of Amigurumi   6

Tools and Materials   8

Reading Patterns   9

Crochet Techniques   10

Finishing Off   14

Creating Happy Gifts   15

Chapter 1: Happy Holidays   18

Chapter 2: Love and Romance   56

Chapter 3: Springtime is Here!   74

Chapter 4: Party Time!   90

Chapter 5: Congratulations!   112

Index   142

Resources   144

Cute, Cute, Cute

Welcome to the Wonderful World of Amigurumi

What is amigurumi?

The word *amigurumi* is a combination of the words *ami* and *nuigurumi*. *Ami* means "knit/crochet" in Japanese and *nuigurumi* means "stuffed toy." Put them together, and you have a crocheted stuffed toy.

No one really knows where amigurumi came from. There have always been handmade toys in Japan. Japan has a rich history in textiles, as we can see in weaving for kimonos, the Japanese traditional costume. But there is no such history of knitting or crochet. The Japanese simply took these Western crafts and, instead of using them for purely functional items like socks and scarves, they started to create little animals. Nowadays, there are hundreds of amigurumi exhibitions and clubs, not only in Japan but all over the world.

The birth of amigurumi may have been greatly influenced by Japanese traditional doll culture, which has a long history. Hina Matsuri, a doll festival in honor of Girls' Day, is celebrated on the third of March every year, just in time for the peach blossoms. The Odairi-sama/Ohina-sama dolls, representing the Emperor and the Empress, are displayed for this festival by each family with a daughter to ensure her future happiness. This set of dolls tends to be handed down from generation to generation with love, respect, and a sense of history. Boys also have a special doll festival in May.

The dolls stay with Japanese children all their lives, lifting their spirits in times of stress and trouble. Amigurumi animals are an extension of this doll culture, brightening up cloudy days and providing a source of comfort at the toughest of times.

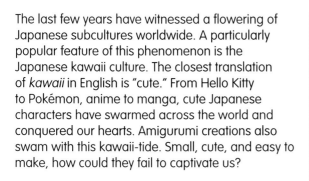

The last few years have witnessed a flowering of Japanese subcultures worldwide. A particularly popular feature of this phenomenon is the Japanese kawaii culture. The closest translation of *kawaii* in English is "cute." From Hello Kitty to Pokémon, anime to manga, cute Japanese characters have swarmed across the world and conquered our hearts. Amigurumi creations also swam with this kawaii-tide. Small, cute, and easy to make, how could they fail to captivate us?

In Japan, people like to keep these animals with them throughout the day. You will see them hanging off bags next to lucky charms, or sitting atop computers and piles of work in the office. Amigurumi characters can comfort and reassure us in this hectic world, secretly saying: "Why don't you take a little break and relax?"

Anyone can master amigurumi, and there are no limits to what you can create. Grab some yarn and crochet hooks, get comfortable by the fire, and start making your own little world.

Tools and Materials

Basic Crochet Kit

Crochet hooks come in a great variety of materials, from wooden and plastic to chunky steel and even ivory. All come in different shapes and sizes. Different countries have different sizing systems—which can be confusing—so always double-check your hook against the conversion charts. Check also that you are using the correct size hook as indicated in the pattern. All of the patterns in this book use a size C (3 mm) crochet hook. However, remember that experimenting with various weights and types of yarn will require different-sized hooks; the important thing is to use a hook that will give a nice tight crochet with the selected yarn.

Knitter's pins with large heads (useful for pinning shapes)

Tapestry needle for sewing up

Split stitch markers for marking the beginnings of rounds.

Tape measure

Sharp scissors

Tweezers to help with stuffing

Embroidery needle for embroidering faces and details.

Embroidery thread

Well-spun yarns are the ideal choice if you want to achieve neat, tidy work.

Fine crochet cotton (lace) thread has a firm texture that is good for very small details. Its thickness is given in numbers, i.e., 5, 10, and so on. The higher the number, the finer the thread.

4-ply yarn is good in general, especially for making smaller items.

Double knit (DK) yarn is good for making large pieces, but make sure the crochet is as tight as possible so the stuffing can't be seen. You can achieve different results in amigurumi depending on what size or type of yarn you use, even when you are working on the same pattern. The thicker the yarn, the bigger your amigurumi will be! Just remember to use the right size hook for your yarn—look on the ball band for this information.

Mohair is good for anything you want to have a fluffy texture.

Fancy yarns, such as tweed-effect wools, lurex, and bouclé yarns, can be used to create texture and add interesting decorative details.

Toy stuffing is the most commonly used material for stuffing amigurumi, but you could also use scraps of yarn for the really tiny parts.

Small wooden sticks for any parts that need a bit of support to stay upright.

Reading Patterns

If this is the first time that you have used crochet patterns, you might feel like you are learning a new language. However, you will soon begin to recognize the abbreviations used in crochet. The abbreviations make patterns shorter and easier to follow.

Let's learn the new crochet language.

Crochet Abbreviations

alt	alternate
approx	approximately
beg	begin/beginning
bet	between
ch	chain stitch
cm	centimeter(s)
col	color
cont	continue
dc	double crochet
dc 2 tog	double crochet 2 stitches together
dec	decrease/decreases/decreasing
foll	follow/follows/following
hdc	half-double crochet
in.	inch(es)
inc	increase/increases/increasing
mm	millimeter(s)
rep	repeat(s)
sc	single crochet
sl st	slip stitch
st(s)	stitch(es)
tog	together
trc	triple crochet
yo	yarn over hook
*	repeat that step

Now, it's time to step into the hook-sizing world.

Both letters and numbers can appear on the packaging of crochet hooks. The metric sizing is the actual measurement of the hook. The letter is the U.S. sizing range. Lettering may vary, so always rely on the metric sizings.

METRIC	U.S.
2.5 mm	B
3 mm	C
3.25 mm	D
3.5 mm	E
4 mm	F
4.25 mm	G
5 mm	H
5.5 mm	I
6 mm	J
7 mm	K
8 mm	L
9 mm	M
10 mm	N
15 mm	P

How to read a Japanese crochet chart

On the Japanese chart, each stitch is shown as follows:

- **Magic ring:** tiny circle in the middle of circular chart   O
- **Single crochet:** cross   x or +
- **Double crochet:** T symbol   T
- **Chain stitch:** tiny oval   o
- **Increasing:** arrow pointing toward the center of the diagram   >
- **Decreasing:** arrow pointing away from the center of the diagram   <
- **Slip stitch:** black oval   ●
- **Back loop:** straight line   —

Follow the chart from the center to the outside, then move to the non-circular part of the chart, if there is one shown above the circular part. Always follow the circular chart counterclockwise.

Crochet Techniques

Crochet is all about mixing really simple techniques with more elaborate flourishes. Once you get the hang of making chains, you are ready to progress to a variety of fancy stitches.

Holding the hook and yarn

Learning how to hold the hook and yarn correctly is the first step to crochet. Most people hold the hook and yarn as they would a pencil or a knife, but you should experiment to find the most comfortable way for you.

Mastering the slipknot

Making a slipknot is the first step in any project. Master the slipknot technique, and you are on your way to super crochet!

Make a loop in the yarn. With your hook, catch the ball end of the yarn and draw it through the loop. Pull firmly on the yarn and hook to tighten the knot and create your first loop.

Making a chain

1. Before making a chain, you need to place the slipknot on a hook. To make a chain, hold the tail end of the yarn with the left hand and bring the yarn over the hook by passing the hook in front of the yarn, under, and around it.

2. Keeping the tension in the yarn taut, draw the hook and yarn through the loop.

3. Pull the yarn, hook it through the hole, and begin again, ensuring that the stitches are fairly loose. Repeat to make the number of chains required. As the chain lengthens, keep hold of the bottom edge to maintain the tension.

How to count a chain

To count the stitches, use the right side of the chain, or the side that has more visible and less twisted "V" shapes, as shown. Do not count the original slip stitch, but count each "V" as one chain.

Making a slip stitch (sl st)

A slip stitch is used to join one stitch to another or a stitch to another point, as in joining a circle, and is usually made by picking up two strands of a stitch.

However, where it is worked into the starting chain, only pick up the back loop.

1. Insert the hook into the back loop of the next stitch and pass yarn over hook (yo), as in the chain stitch.

2. Draw yarn through both loops of stitch and repeat.

The magic ring: working in the round

There are two ways to start circular crochet. One is with a chain and another is with a loop. A loop, or magic ring, is the more usual way to make amigurumi. This way of working in the round ensures that there is no hole in the middle of the work, as there is with a chain ring, because the central hole is adjustable and can be pulled tightly closed.

Let's make a magic ring

This will be the first round of your amigurumi, so you need to master it!

1. Make a loop by wrapping the yarn twice onto your forefinger, with the tail end of the yarn on the right, the ball end on the left.

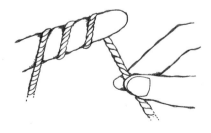

2. Pull the ball end through the loop (steady your work with your hand).

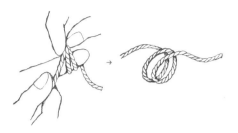

3. Make one chain (ch) through the loop on the hook you have drawn through to steady the round.

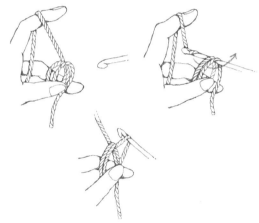

4. Work as many single crochet (sc), or whatever stitch you are using, into the loop as is required by the pattern.

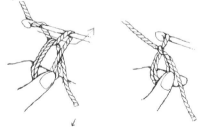

5. Pull the last stitch out long enough so that it won't come undone. Find out which loop will be tightened first by pulling one of the loops.

6. Pull this loop as tight as you can.

7. Pull the tail end of the yarn to tighten up the whole loop. Now you have no hole in the middle of the first round.

Completing the magic ring: first round

Insert the hook into the first stitch of a magic ring and pull the yarn through all the way.

This is called "slip stitch" (sl st).

Start the second round

To crochet a flat circle, you need to keep working in the round with increasing stitches.

1. Make one chain (ch). Insert the hook into the first stitch of a circle, put the yarn over the hook (yo), and then draw the yarn through the loop. This is called single crochet (sc). In amigurumi, this is the technique you will use the most.

2. Add one more sc into the same stitch. This is called increasing (inc).

Repeat 1 and 2 into every stitch and you will finish the second round with twice the number of stitches.

On the second round, increase in alternate stitches.

Third round: 1 sc into each of the next 2 stitches, 2 sc into the next one. Repeat.

Fourth round: 1 sc into each of the next 3 stitches, 2 sc into the next one. Repeat.

The more rounds you go, the more stitches you need to make between increases.

Making a chain ring

1. Work a chain as long as required by the pattern.

2. Join the last chain to the first with a slip stitch (sl st). Begin the first round by working into each chain stitch.

Variety of stitches

Single crochet (sc): the main stitch used for amigurumi

1. Insert the hook, front to back, into the next stitch. Yo.

2. Draw through one loop to front; there should be two loops on the hook. Yo.

3. Draw through both loops to complete single crochet.

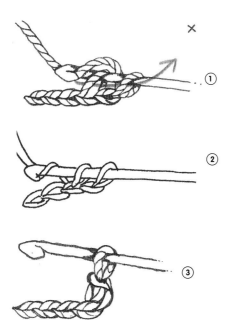

Double crochet (dc)

This makes a more open fabric as the stitches are taller.

1. Wrap the yarn over the hook (yo) from back to front. Insert the hook into the next stitch, from front to back. Yo again and draw through the stitch.

2. There should be three loops on the hook. Yo and pull through two loops.

3. There should be two loops on the hook. Yo and pull through the remaining two loops.

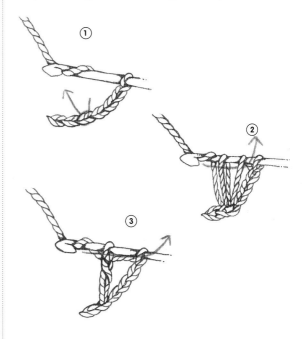

Half-double crochet (hdc)

The half-double is simply that: half of a double crochet. Therefore, the stitch is slightly shorter than double crochet. In step 2 of double crochet, pull through all the remaining loops in one movement.

Finishing Off

When you've finished crocheting your lovely presents, fastening off is the next most important step. After that, all you need to do is fill it with stuffing and stitch the parts together.

Here are some useful things to remember

When you fasten off the end of a part that is going to be stitched to another part, leave a long tail for sewing the two together. Do not weave this end in.

Connect two pieces by taking stitches alternately from each piece and fastening them securely.

Fastening off

1. After working the last stitch, snip off the yarn from the ball, leaving a length of a few centimeters to weave in.

2. Draw through the last loop, pulling tightly to fasten.

Weaving in ends

1. Use the hook to draw the yarn through at least five stitches, weaving the yarn over and under as you go to secure the yarn and ensure it does not work free.

2. Snip off the excess yarn.

When fastening off, leave openings for stuffing where appropriate. Stuff firmly, sew up gaps, and embroider details as shown in the illustrations.

Creating Happy Gifts

There aren't really any hard-and-fast rules when it comes to designing amigurumi. Once you've mastered the basic stitches and practiced the technique of working in the round, you're bound to be inspired to start inventing your own crocheted creations. In this book, you will find 25 patterns for all sorts of special events—from holidays to romantic occasions to birthdays and personal victories. But there are so many more special occasions out there to inspire you—so get out the crochet hook and start creating!

Developing a design

Amigurumi makes the perfect gift for any affair, and it can be easily adapted to suit your particular celebration.

Designs in this book are as diverse as a dragon to mark the Chinese New Year, Santa Claus and Rudolph the Red-Nose Reindeer, Love Birds for an anniversary, as well as ideas for a school graduation, but amigurumi isn't limited to these ideas alone. The best way to make your own one-of-a-kind design is to get inspired by browsing the Internet or through books to find that one image that speaks to you—and then create it in crochet!

Don't be put off by my complicated designs—remember, you can make things in several parts and then stitch them all together later. And don't be afraid to try shapes other than round.

Sketching

When I have an idea, I start by making a sketch. It might be a pencil drawing or something more complicated, with colors added. You don't have to be good at drawing to do this; sometimes just a brief drawing of a shape and a little scribble of some details are enough to help you envisage the finished shape of your amigurumi, and to help you get started with the stitching.

Choosing materials

There are lots of lovely brightly colored holiday motifs, so there is plenty of opportunity to get out some fun yarns. Bright greens, rosy reds, and sunshine yellows can all make an appearance when celebrating our favorite occasions.

The choice of materials is endless. By playing with a variety of materials, you'll discover interesting differences in your finished result. Experiment with fancy yarns—yarns with touches of glitter and fluff—to create eye-catching textures.

Making shapes

This section will show you how to create some of the basic shapes for your projects. A lot of these shapes can be twisted and folded, or stitched to other shapes to create new ones.

Once you've mastered these, you can change the shapes to create all kinds of different celebratory objects.

Teardrop shapes

This type of shape is really simple. Just make a disc in the size you want, then continue with sc until the section is the length you require.

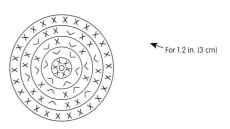

← For 1.2 in. (3 cm)

Disc shapes

These are very simple to make. Start with the magic circle and then keep increasing stitches until the disc is the size you want. To make circular treats, make two discs, stitch together, and stuff. To make semicircular items, fold a disc in half before stitching and stuffing.

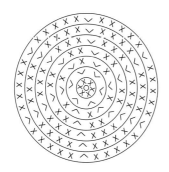

Ball shapes

Start with a disc shape, and then keep increasing stitches until the disc is the size of sphere you want to make. Continue for a couple of rounds without shaping, and then start decreasing.

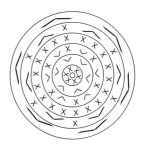

Rectangles and squares

These are probably the easiest shapes to make. Start with a basic chain and then work crochet stitches along it. Turn the work at the end of the row and then work back along it. Keep going until you've got a piece the size you want. Squares and rectangles can be folded, bent, or rolled into different shapes.

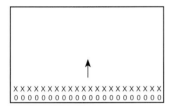

Rhomboid shapes

This four-sided shape looks like a sloping rectangle. It's useful for making twisted shapes. Start with a foundation chain, as you would for a square or rectangle and then decrease by two stitches (sc 2 tog) at the beginning of the first row, and increase (2 sc into same st) at the end of the row. On the next row, increase at the beginning and decrease at the end. Continue working, increasing and decreasing in the same way until the shape is as big as you need.

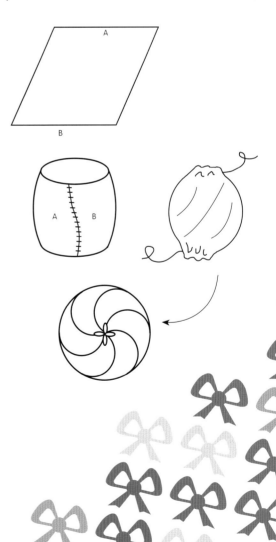

Rectangles with curved corners

To make this type of shape, start with a chain and work one row of stitches, just as for an ordinary square or rectangle. Then, instead of turning the work and crocheting in rows, you work into the first chain, making stitches in the underside of the chain. To make sure the shape lies flat, you need to make at least three stitches in the first and last chains of the foundation chain.

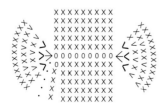

Chapter 1

Happy
Holidays

Oh Christmas Tree!

Get the festivities started with a bit of special sparkle. Make a magical Christmas tree and deck its boughs with some shiny little baubles. Finish off this favorite decoration with a smiley super-star.

Size

Height with star: 6.3 in. (16 cm)

Materials

HOOK SIZE: C (3 mm)

YARN:

Green in different shades for the tree

Yellow for the star

Purple for the star faces

OTHER MATERIALS:

Toy stuffing

Small star-shaped beads for decoration

Gold ribbon or wrapping tape

Structure

The Christmas tree is made in three parts: the first is the tree, the second is the base, the third is frilly lengths, which are coiled around the base to represent the leaves.

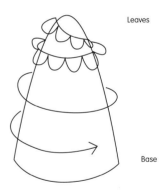

Tree

Using green yarn, make a magic ring as follows.

Make a loop with tail end of yarn on right, keeping ball end on left. Pull the ball end through loop. Make one chain through loop on hook you have drawn through to steady the circle. Work 6 sc into the circle and complete with sl st into the first sc. See also page 13.

1st round: 2 sc into each sc. (12 sts)

2nd–4th rounds: 1 sc into each sc.

5th round: [1 sc into next sc, 2 sc into foll 1 sc] 6 times. (18 sts)

6th–8th rounds: 1 sc into each sc.

9th round: [1 sc into each of next 2 sc, 2 sc into foll 1 sc] 6 times. (24 sts)

10th–15th rounds: 1 sc into each sc.

16th round: [1 sc into each of next 3 sc, 2 sc into foll sc] 6 times. (30 sts)

17th–22nd rounds: 1 sc into each sc.

23rd round: [1 sc into each of next 4 sc, 2 sc into foll sc] 6 times. (36 sts)

24th–30th rounds: 1 sc into each sc.

Fasten off.

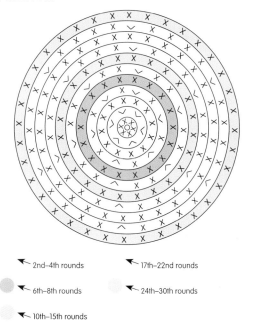

    2nd–4th rounds   17th–22nd rounds

    6th–8th rounds   24th–30th rounds

    10th–15th rounds

Base

Using green yarn, make a magic ring as for the tree.

1st round: 2 sc into each sc. (12 sts)

2nd round: [1 sc into next sc, 2 sc into foll 1 sc] 6 times. (18 sts)

3rd round: [1 sc into each of next 2 sc, 2 sc into foll 1 sc] 6 times. (24 sts)

4th round: [1 sc into each of next 3 sc, 2 sc into foll sc] 6 times. (30 sts)

5th round: [1 sc into each of next 4 sc, 2 sc into foll sc] 6 times. (36 sts)

Fasten off.

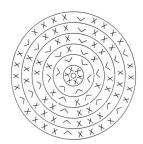

Leaves

picot = 3 ch, sl st into base of the 3 ch just worked.

Using green yarn, make a ch a multiple of 4 ch.

1st row: 1 dc into the fourth ch from the hook, picot, 1 dc into base of last dc, picot, *1 ch, skip 1 ch, 1 sc into next ch, 1 ch, skip 1 ch, into next ch [1 dc, picot] 5 times; repeat from * until 4 ch remain, 1 ch, skip 1 ch, 1 sc into next ch, 1 ch, skip 1 ch, into last ch [1 dc, picot] 3 times.

Fasten off.

Repeat using different shades of green yarn worked to varying lengths.

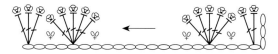

Star (make 2)

Using yellow yarn, make a magic ring as for the tree.

1st round: Working into the center of the ring, [1 sc, 2 ch, 1 dc, 2 ch, 1 sc] 4 times, 1 sc, 2 ch, 1 dc, 2 ch, sl st into first sc of the round.

2nd round: *1 ch, skip 1 ch, 1 sc into next ch, [1 sc, 1 hdc] into next dc, 2 ch, 2 sc into post of last hdc, 1 sc into the next ch, 1 ch, sl st into next ch; repeat from * 4 times more.

Fasten off.

Making up

With your preferred side facing out and using matching yarn, sew the two pieces together around most of the outer edge, fill with toy stuffing, and complete the seam. Then, using the photographs as reference, and purple yarn, embroider on cute faces!

Finishing

Pin the base to the tree and sew the two pieces together around most of the outer edge, fill with toy stuffing, and complete the seam.

Using the photographs as reference and matching yarn, stitch the leaves and star to the tree. Decorate the tree with gold ribbon and small star-shaped beads to add Christmas magic.

Hello Santa

If you've been good, very-very good, then maybe this special Santa will pay you a visit. So don't forget to be on your best behavior all year round if you want to see this jolly Christmas character.

Size

Height: 8.7 in. (22 cm)

Materials

HOOK SIZE: C (3 mm)

YARN:

Flesh-colored for the head and nose

Cream for the hair, beard, and bobble

Red for the cheeks, hat, arms, legs, and body

Black for the belt

Yellow for the belt

OTHER MATERIALS:

Toy stuffing

2 toy safety eyes, .32 in. (8 mm)

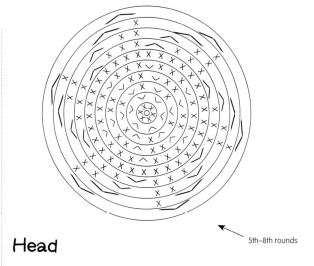

5th–8th rounds

Head

Using flesh-colored yarn, make a magic ring as follows.

Make a loop with tail end of yarn on right, keeping ball end on left. Pull the ball end through loop. Make one chain through loop on hook you have drawn through to steady the circle. Work 6 sc into the circle and complete with sl st into the first sc. See also page 13.

1st round: 2 sc into each sc. (12 sts)

2nd round: [1 sc into next sc, 2 sc into foll 1 sc] 6 times. (18 sts)

3rd round: [1 sc into each of next 2 sc, 2 sc into foll 1 sc] 6 times. (24 sts)

4th round: [1 sc into each of next 3 sc, 2 sc into foll sc] 6 times. (30 sts)

5th–8th rounds: 1 sc into each sc.

9th round: [1 sc into each of next 3 sc, sc 2 tog] 6 times. (24 sts)

10th round: [1 sc into each of next 2 sc, sc 2 tog] 6 times. (18 sts)

Secure the toy eyes approximately 7 sts apart on the sixth round and stuff the head with toy stuffing.

11th round: [1 sc into next sc, sc 2 tog] 6 times. (12 sts)

12th round: [sc 2 tog] 6 times. (6 sts)

Fasten off.

Body

Using red yarn, make a magic ring as for the head.

1st round: 2 sc into each sc. (12 sts)

2nd round: [1 sc into next sc, 2 sc into foll sc] 6 times. (18 sts)

3rd round: [1 sc into each of next 2 sc, 2 sc into foll sc] 6 times. (24 sts)

4th round: [1 sc into each of next 3 sc, 2 sc into foll sc] 6 times. (30 sts)

5th round: [1 sc into each of next 4 sc, 2 sc into foll sc] 6 times. (36 sts)

6th–10th rounds: 1 sc into each sc.

11th round: [1 sc into each of next 4 sc, sc 2 tog] 6 times. (30 sts)

12th round: 1 sc into each sc.

13th round: [1 sc into each of next 3 sc, sc 2 tog] 6 times. (24 sts)

14th round: 1 sc into each sc.

15th round: [1 sc into each of next 2 sc, sc 2 tog] 6 times. (18 sts)

16th round: 1 sc into each sc.

17th round: [1 sc into each of next 1 sc, sc 2 tog] 6 times. (12 sts)

Fasten off.

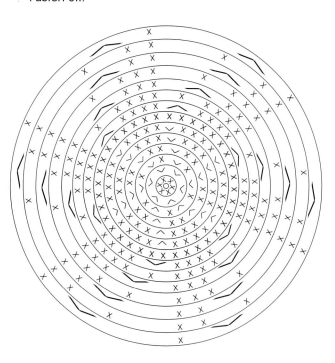

6th–10th rounds

Nose

Using flesh-colored yarn, make a magic ring as for the head.

1st round: 2 sc into each sc. (12 sts)

2nd–3rd rounds: 1 sc into each sc.

Fasten off.

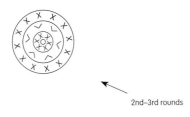

2nd–3rd rounds

Cheeks (make 2)

Using red yarn, make a magic ring as for the head.

Work as for nose.

Hair

Work each sc with long fur stitch loops worked as follows.

Insert the hook into the place or stitch directed, hook both sets of strands hanging down on either side of the raised index finger to create a loop, draw all the strands through the fabric, remove the index finger from the loop but hold the loop firmly against the fabric, wrap the yarn around the hook, and draw it through all the loops on the hook. Firmly pull on the loop to draw it tight.

Using cream, make a magic ring as for the head.

1st round: 2 sc into each sc. (12 sts)

2nd round: [1 sc into next sc, 2 sc into foll sc] 6 times. (18 sts)

3rd round: [1 sc into each of next 2 sc, 2 sc into foll sc] 6 times. (24 sts)

Fasten off.

Beard

Work each sc with long fur stitch loops worked as above for the hair.

Using cream yarn, make 6 ch.

1st row: 1 sc into the second ch from the hook, 1 sc into each ch, turn. (5 sts)

2nd–4th rows: 1 ch, 1 sc into each sc, turn.

Fasten off.

```
O X X X X X
 X X X X X O
  O O O O O
```

Hat

Using red yarn, make a magic ring as for the head.

1st round: 1 sc into each sc.

2nd round: 2 sc into each sc. (12 sts)

3rd–5th rounds: 1 sc into each sc.

6th round: [1 sc into next sc, 2 sc into foll sc] 6 times. (18 sts)

7th–8th rounds: 1 sc into each sc.

Fasten off.

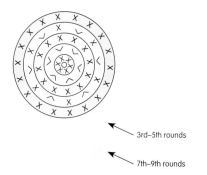

3rd–5th rounds

7th–9th rounds

Hat bobble

Using cream yarn, make a magic ring as for the head.

1st–2nd rounds: 1 sc into each sc.

Fasten off.

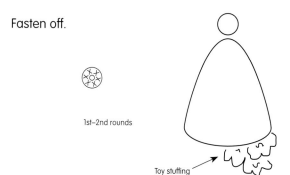

1st–2nd rounds

Toy stuffing

Legs (make 2)

Using red yarn, make a magic ring as for the head.

1st round: 2 sc into each sc. (12 sts)

2nd–7th rounds: 1 sc into each sc.

Fasten off.

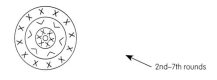

2nd–7th rounds

Arms (make 2)

Using red yarn, make a magic ring as for the head.

1st round: 2 sc into each sc. (12 sts)

2nd–10th rounds: 1 sc into each sc.

Fasten off.

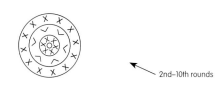

2nd–10th rounds

Making up

Using the photographs as reference and matching yarn, stitch the beard, cheeks, and nose to the face and the hair and a hat with toy stuffing to the head. Attach the bobble to the hat.

Fill the body, arms, and legs with toy stuffing. Attach the head, arms, and legs to the body.

To make the belt, using black yarn, make a ch long enough to go around the body.

1st row: 1 sc into the second ch from the hook, 1 sc into each ch, turn.

2nd row: 1 ch, 1 sc into each sc, turn.

Fasten off.

Using yellow yarn and straight stitches, embroider a buckle onto the belt.

Red-nose Reindeer

Santa wouldn't be able to do his gift-giving job without his happy helpers, and no one is more important than the reindeers that pull his sleigh. Crochet this cute red-nose critter to be your own special Christmas companion.

Size

Height: 8.3 in. (21 cm)

Materials

HOOK SIZE: C (3 mm)

YARN:

Brown for the head, ears, snout, jaw, chest, body, legs, and tail

Light brown for the antlers and feet

Red for the nose

OTHER MATERIALS:

Toy stuffing

2 toy safety eyes, .32 in. (8 mm)

Structure

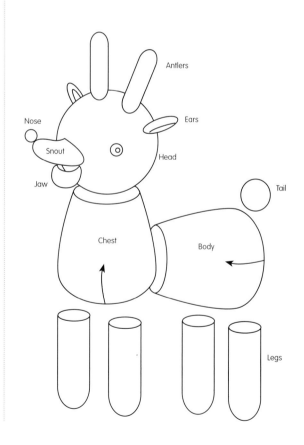

Head

Using brown yarn, make a magic ring as follows.

Make a loop with tail end of yarn on right, keeping ball end on left. Pull the ball end through loop. Make one chain through loop on hook you have drawn through to steady the circle. Work 6 sc into the circle and complete with sl st into the first sc. See also page 13.

1st round: 2 sc into each sc. (12 sts)

2nd round: [1 sc into next sc, 2 sc into foll 1 sc] 6 times. (18 sts)

3rd round: [1 sc into each of next 2 sc, 2 sc into foll 1 sc] 6 times. (24 sts)

4th round: [1 sc into each of next 3 sc, 2 sc into foll sc] 6 times. (30 sts)

5th–8th rounds: 1 sc into each sc.

9th round: [1 sc into each of next 3 sc, sc 2 tog] 6 times. (24 sts)

10th round: [1 sc into each of next 2 sc, sc 2 tog] 6 times. (18 sts)

Secure the toy safety eyes approximately 6 sts apart on the sixth round and fill the head with toy stuffing.

11th round: [1 sc into next sc, sc 2 tog] 6 times. (12 sts)

12th round: [sc 2 tog] 6 times. (6 sts)

Fasten off.

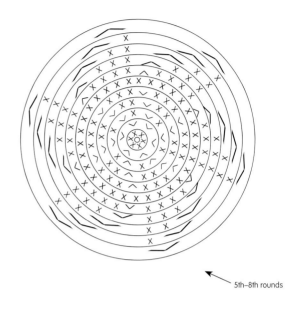

5th–8th rounds

Chest

Using brown yarn, make a magic ring as for the head.

1st round: 2 sc into each sc. (12 sts)

2nd round: [1 sc into next sc, 2 sc into foll sc] 6 times. (18 sts)

3rd round: [1 sc into each of next 2 sc, 2 sc into foll sc] 6 times. (24 sts)

4th round: [1 sc into each of next 3 sc, 2 sc into foll sc] 6 times. (30 sts)

5th–9th rounds: 1 sc into each sc.

10th round: [1 sc into each of next 3 sc, sc 2 tog] 6 times. (24 sts)

11th round: 1 sc into each sc.

12th round: [1 sc into each of next 2 sc, sc 2 tog] 6 times. (18 sts)

13th–14th rounds: 1 sc into each sc.

Fasten off.

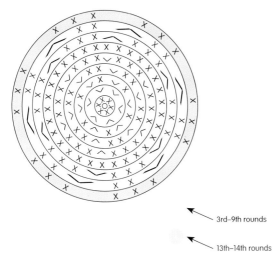

3rd–9th rounds

13th–14th rounds

Body

Using brown yarn, make a magic ring as for the head.

1st round: 2 sc into each sc. (12 sts)

2nd round: [1 sc into next sc, 2 sc into foll sc] 6 times. (18 sts)

3rd round: [1 sc into each of next 2 sc, 2 sc into foll sc] 6 times. (24 sts)

5th–9th rounds: 1 sc into each sc.

Fasten off.

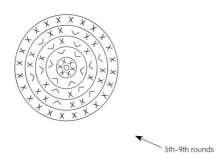

5th–9th rounds

Legs (make 4)

Using light brown yarn, make a magic ring as for the head.

1st round: 2 sc into each sc. (12 sts)

2nd–4th rounds: 1 sc into each sc.

Fasten off light brown yarn, join in brown.

5nd–12th rounds: 1 sc into each sc.

Fasten off.

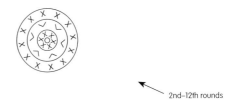

2nd–12th rounds

Snout

Using brown yarn, make a magic ring as for the head.

1st round: 2 sc into each sc. (12 sts)

2nd–4th rounds: 1 sc into each sc.

5th round: [1 sc into next sc, 2 sc into foll sc] 6 times. (18 sts)

6th–7th rounds: 1 sc into each sc.

Fasten off.

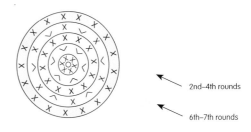

2nd–4th rounds

6th–7th rounds

Nose

Using red yarn, make a magic ring as for the head.

1st round: 2 sc into each sc. (12 sts)

2nd–4th rounds: 1 sc into each sc.

Fasten off.

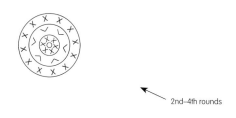

2nd–4th rounds

Mouth

Using brown yarn, make a magic ring as for the head.

1st round: 2 sc into each sc. (12 sts)

2nd round: [1 sc into next sc, 2 sc into foll sc] 6 times. (18 sts)

3rd–4th rounds: 1 sc into each sc.

Fasten off.

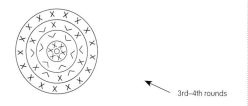

3rd–4th rounds

Ears (make 2)

Using brown yarn, make a magic ring as for the head.

1st round: 2 sc into each sc. (12 sts)

2nd round: [1 sc into next sc, 2 sc into foll sc] 6 times. (18 sts)

Fasten off.

Antlers (make 2)

Using light brown yarn, make a magic ring as for the head.

1st–8th rounds: 1 sc into each sc.

Fasten off.

1st–8th rounds

Tail

Using brown yarn, make a magic ring as for the head.

1st round: 2 sc into each sc. (12 sts)

2nd–5th rounds: 1 sc into each sc.

Fasten off.

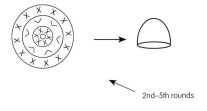

2nd–5th rounds

Making up

Fill the head, snout, and nose with toy stuffing. Sew nose to snout. Pinch a small section of each ear piece and stitch in place. Using the photographs as reference and matching yarn, stitch the antlers, ears snout, mouth, and nose to the head. Fill the chest, body, and legs with toy stuffing.

Attach the head and body to the chest. Pin the legs to the body and chest sections, and adjust their position as required in order for the reindeer to stand. Stitch the legs in place and attach the tail.

Angel Girl

Hark the happy angels sing! It's Christmas time! This glittery angel girl is sure to brighten up anyone's yuletide celebrations. Pop her on the tree and she can outshine all the other decorations.

Size

Height: 8 in. (20 cm)

Materials

HOOK SIZE: C (3 mm)

YARN:

Flesh-colored for the head and nose

White and cream for the body

Cream for the legs

Blue Lurex or sparkly yarn for the cape and halo

Red for the cheeks

Yellow for the hair

OTHER MATERIALS:

Toy stuffing

2 toy safety eyes, .32 in. (8 mm)

Structure

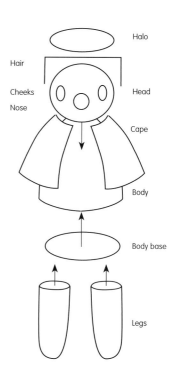

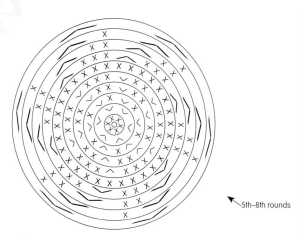

5th–8th rounds

Head

Using flesh-colored yarn, make a magic ring as follows.

Make a loop with tail end of yarn on right, keeping ball end on left. Pull the ball end through loop. Make one chain through loop on hook you have drawn through to steady the circle. Work 6 sc into the circle and complete with sl st into the first sc. See also page 13.

1st round: 2 sc into each sc. (12 sts)

2nd round: [1 sc into next sc, 2 sc into foll 1 sc] 6 times. (18 sts)

3rd round: [1 sc into each of next 2 sc, 2 sc into foll 1 sc] 6 times. (24 sts)

4th round: [1 sc into each of next 3 sc, 2 sc into foll sc] 6 times. (30 sts)

5th–8th rounds: 1 sc into each sc.

9th round: [1 sc into each of next 3 sc, sc 2 tog] 6 times. (24 sts)

10th round: [1 sc into each of next 2 sc, sc 2 tog] 6 times. (18 sts)

Secure the toy safety eyes approximately 6 sts apart on the sixth round and fill the head with toy stuffing.

11th round: [1 sc into next sc, sc 2 tog] 6 times. (12 sts)

12th round: [sc 2 tog] 6 times. (6 sts)

Fasten off.

Body

Using white and cream yarn stranded together, make a magic ring as for the head.

1st round: 2 sc into each sc. (12 sts)

2nd round: [1 sc into next sc, 2 sc into foll sc] 6 times. (18 sts)

3rd round: [1 sc into each of next 2 sc, 2 sc into foll sc] 6 times. (24 sts)

4th round: [1 sc into each of next 3 sc, 2 sc into foll sc] 6 times. (30 sts)

5th–14th rounds: 1 sc into each sc.

Fasten off.

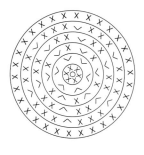

5th–14th rounds

Body base

Using cream yarn, make a magic ring as for the head.

1st round: 2 sc into each sc. (12 sts)

2nd round: [1 sc into next sc, 2 sc into foll sc] 6 times. (18 sts)

3rd round: [1 sc into each of next 2 sc, 2 sc into foll sc] 6 times. (24 sts)

4th round: [1 sc into each of next 3 sc, 2 sc into foll sc] 6 times. (30 sts)

5th round: 1 sc into each sc.

Fasten off.

Legs (make 2)

Using cream yarn, make a magic ring as for the head.

1st round: 2 sc into each sc. (12 sts)

2nd round: [1 sc into next sc, 2 sc into foll sc] 6 times. (18 sts)

Work 1 sc into each sc until the piece measures 2 in. (5 cm).

Fasten off.

2 in. (5 cm)

Cheeks (make 2)

Using red yarn, make a magic ring as for the head.

Fasten off.

Nose

Using flesh-colored yarn, make a magic ring as for the head.

1st–2nd rounds: 1 sc into each sc. (6 sts)

Fasten off.

1st–2nd rounds

Cape

Using blue Lurex yarn, make 30 ch.

1st row: 1 sc into the eleventh ch from the hook, [5 ch, skip 3 ch, 1 sc into next ch] 4 times, 3 ch, 1 dc into last ch, turn.

2nd row: 7 ch, skip ch-sp, 1 sc into next ch-sp, [5 ch, skip 3 ch, 1 sc into next ch] 4 times, 3 ch, 1 dc into the same ch-sp as last sc, turn.

Repeat the last row three more times.

Fasten off.

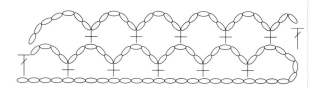

Halo

2 dc-bobble = [wrap the yarn around the hook, insert the hook into fourth ch from hook, wrap yarn around hook, draw yarn through ch, wrap yarn around hook, draw yarn through two loops on hook] twice, wrap yarn around hook, draw yarn through all loops on the hook.

Using blue Lurex yarn, make 4 ch.

1st row: 2 dc-bobble, [4 ch, 2 dc-bobble] 9 times.

Fasten off.

Making up

Using the photographs as reference and matching yarn, stitch the cheeks and nose to the face.

To make hair, wrap yellow yarn around a piece of cardboard 5.5 in. (14 cm) wide, approximately ten times, secure with a loop of matching yarn, and leave long yarn-ends for sewing to the head. Fold each section in half and attach to the head.

Attach the halo, allowing some hair to appear to be covering the halo.

Using the structure diagram and photographs as reference, stuff and assemble the body and leg pieces.

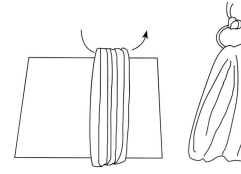

Wow Wow Candles

Let in the light and illuminate your winter celebrations with these cheery candles. Set them on the festive table and they will shine and shimmer throughout the dark nights. Happy Hanukkah!

Size

Heights: 4.3 in. (11 cm); 5.3 in. (13.5 cm); 6.3 in. (16 cm)

Materials

HOOK size: C (3 mm)

YARN:

White for the wax

Red for the flame

OTHER MATERIALS:

Cardboard

Toy stuffing

3rd round onward until the desired height is reached

Candle body

Make candles of three different heights (for your menorah make x3 sets)!

Using white yarn, make a magic ring as follows.

Make a loop with tail end of yarn on right, keeping ball end on left. Pull the ball end through loop. Make one chain through loop on hook you have drawn through to steady the circle. Work 6 sc into the circle and complete with sl st into the first sc. See also page 13.

1st round: 2 sc into each sc. (12 sts)

2nd round: [1 sc into next sc, 2 sc into foll 1 sc] 6 times. (18 sts)

3rd round: 1 sc into each sc.

Repeat the last round until the desired height is reached.

Fasten off.

Candle body base

Using white yarn, make a magic ring as for the candle body.

1st round: 2 sc into each sc. (12 sts)

2nd round: [1 sc into next sc, 2 sc into foll sc] 6 times. (18 sts)

Fasten off.

Wax collar

Using white yarn, make a magic ring as for the candle body.

1st round: 2 sc into each sc. (12 sts)

2nd round: [1 sc into next sc, 2 sc into foll sc] 6 times. (18 sts)

3rd round: Work ch lengths and sc, hdc, and dc sts, randomly for melting wax effect.

Flame

Using red yarn, make a magic ring as for the candle body.

1st round: 2 sc into each sc. (12 sts)

2nd round: [1 sc into next sc, 2 sc into foll 1 sc] 6 times. (18 sts)

3rd–5th rounds: 1 sc into each sc.

6th round: [1 sc into next sc, sc 2 tog] 6 times. (12 sts)

7th round: [sc 2 tog] 6 times. (6 sts)

Fasten off.

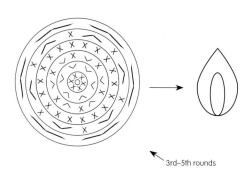

3rd–5th rounds

Making up

Cut the cardboard to the same length as the candle body and roll it into a cylinder shape. Insert the cardboard roll and toy stuffing into the candle body.

Using the photographs on page 43 as reference and matching yarn, stitch the candle body base, the wax collar, and an unstuffed flame to the candle body.

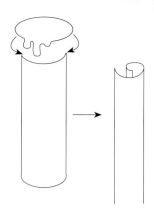

Thanksgiving Turkey

As leaves turn gold and start to fall, it's the traditional time to celebrate the end of summer goodness. This trim little turkey is the perfect guest at any feast and makes the ideal gift to say a special thank you to best friends.

Size

Height: 4.3 in. (11 cm)

Materials

HOOK SIZE: C (3 mm)

YARN:

Brown for the head and body

Yellow for the beak and tail

Red for wattle and tail

OTHER MATERIALS:

Toy stuffing

2 toy safety eyes, .32 in. (8 mm)

Structure

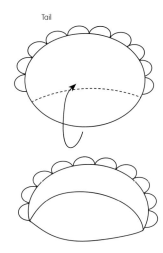

Head

Using brown yarn, make a magic ring as follows.

Make a loop with tail end of yarn on right, keeping ball end on left. Pull the ball end through loop. Make one chain through loop on hook you have drawn through to steady the circle. Work 6 sc into the circle and complete with sl st into the first sc. See also page 13.

1st round: 2 sc into each sc. (12 sts)

2nd round: [1 sc into next sc, 2 sc into foll 1 sc] 6 times. (18 sts)

3rd round: [1 sc into each of next 2 sc, 2 sc into foll 1 sc] 6 times. (24 sts)

4th–7th rounds: 1 sc into each sc.

8th round: [1 sc into each of next 2 sc, sc 2 tog] 6 times. (18 sts)

Secure the toy safety eyes approximately 4 sts apart on the sixth round and fill the head with toy stuffing.

9th round: [1 sc into next sc, sc 2 tog] 6 times. (12 sts)

10th round: [sc 2 tog] 6 times. (6 sts)

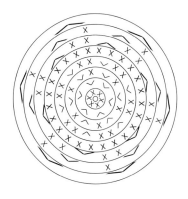

4th–7th rounds

Body

Using brown yarn, make a magic ring as for the head.

1st round: 2 sc into each sc. (12 sts)

2nd round: [1 sc into next sc, 2 sc into foll sc] 6 times. (18 sts)

3rd round: [1 sc into each of next 2 sc, 2 sc into foll sc] 6 times. (24 sts)

4th–7th rounds: 1 sc into each sc.

8th round: [1 sc into each of next 2 sc, sc 2 tog] 6 times. (18 sts)

9th–11th rounds: 1 sc into each sc.

12th round: [1 sc into next sc, sc 2 tog] 6 times. (12 sts)

13th round: 1 sc into each sc.

Fasten off.

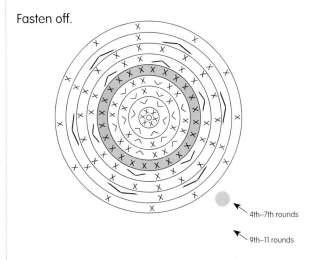

4th–7th rounds

9th–11 rounds

Tail

Using red yarn double stranded, make a magic ring as for the head.

1st round: 2 sc into each sc. (12 sts)

2nd round: [1 sc into next sc, 2 sc into foll sc] 6 times. (18 sts)

3rd round: [1 sc into each of next 2 sc, 2 sc into foll sc] 6 times. (24 sts)

4th round: [1 sc into each of next 3 sc, 2 sc into foll sc] 6 times. (30 sts)

5th round: [1 sc into each of next 4 sc, 2 sc into foll sc] 6 times. (36 sts)

Fasten off red yarn, join in yellow yarn.

6th round: *1 sc into next sc, into the foll stitch [1 hdc, 3 dc, 1 hdc]; repeat from * 9 more times, 1 sc into the next sc.

Fasten off.

Beak

Using yellow yarn, make a magic ring as for the head.

1st round: 2 sc into each sc. (12 sts)

2nd–4th rounds: 1 sc into each sc.

Fasten off.

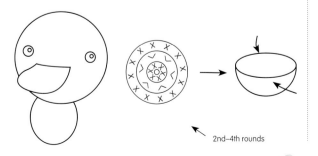

2nd–4th rounds

Wattle

Using red yarn, make a magic ring as for the head.

1st round: 2 sc into each sc. (12 sts)

2nd round: [1 sc into next sc, 2 sc into foll sc] 6 times. (18 sts)

3rd–6th rounds: 1 sc into each sc.

3rd–6th rounds

Making up

Using the structure diagram and photographs as reference and matching yarn, stuff and assemble the body and head pieces. Attach the beak and wattle to the face. Fold the tail as shown in the structure diagram and attach to the body.

New Year Dragon

Red is the color of good fortune in China, and New Year is the time to give presents. So ensure you have a lucky year ahead, and make this friendly beast to welcome in the Year of the Dragon!

Size

Height: 5.1 in. (13 cm)

Materials

HOOK SIZE: C (3 mm)

YARN:

Red for the head, nose, neck, body, and tail

Yellow for the arms, legs, feet, and spine

Green for the ears

OTHER MATERIALS:

Toy stuffing

2 toy safety eyes, .32 in. (8 mm)

Structure

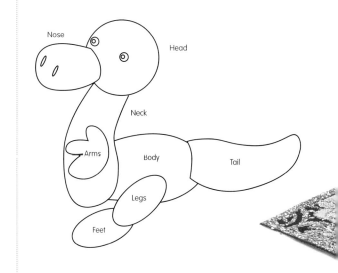

Head

Using red yarn, make a magic ring as follows.

Make a loop with tail end of yarn on right, keeping ball end on left. Pull the ball end through loop. Make one chain through loop on hook you have drawn through to steady the circle. Work 6 sc into the circle and complete with sl st into the first sc. See also page 13.

1st round: 2 sc into each sc. (12 sts)

2nd round: [1 sc into next sc, 2 sc into foll 1 sc] 6 times. (18 sts)

3rd round: [1 sc into each of next 2 sc, 2 sc into foll 1 sc] 6 times. (24 sts)

4th–7th rounds: 1 sc into each sc.

8th round: [1 sc into each of next 2 sc, sc 2 tog] 6 times. (18 sts)

Secure the toy safety eyes approximately 5 sts apart on the third round and fill the head with toy stuffing.

9th round: [1 sc into next sc, sc 2 tog] 6 times. (12 sts)

10th round: [sc 2 tog] 6 times. (6 sts)

Fasten off.

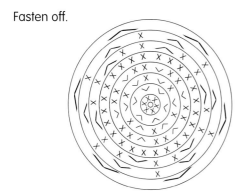

4th–7th rounds

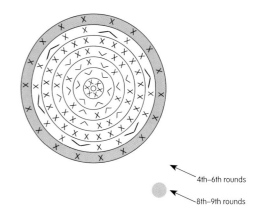

4th–6th rounds

8th–9th rounds

Nose

Using red yarn, make a magic ring as for the head.

1st round: 2 sc into each sc. (12 sts)

2nd round: [1 sc into next sc, 2 sc into foll sc] 6 times. (18 sts)

3rd round: [1 sc into each of next 2 sc, 2 sc into foll sc] 6 times. (24 sts)

4th–6th rounds: 1 sc into each sc.

7th round: [1 sc into each of next 2 sc, sc 2 tog] 6 times. (18 sts)

8th–9th rounds: 1 sc into each sc.

Fasten off.

Neck

Using red yarn, make a magic ring as for the head.

1st round: 2 sc into each sc. (12 sts)

2nd round: [1 sc into next sc, 2 sc into foll sc] 6 times. (18 sts)

3rd–20th rounds: 1 sc into each sc.

Fasten off.

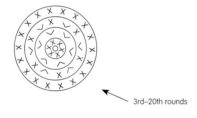

3rd–20th rounds

Body

Using red yarn, make a magic ring as for the head.

1st round: 2 sc into each sc. (12 sts)

2nd round: [1 sc into next sc, 2 sc into foll sc] 6 times. (18 sts)

3rd–10th rounds: 1 sc into each sc.

Fasten off.

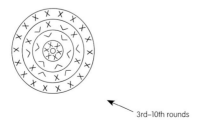

3rd–10th rounds

Tail

Using red yarn, make a magic ring as for the head.

1st round: 2 sc into each sc. (12 sts)

2nd–5th rounds: 1 sc into each sc.

6th round: [1 sc into next sc, 2 sc into foll sc] 6 times. (18 sts)

7th–16th rounds: 1 sc into each sc.

Fasten off.

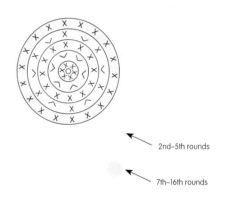

2nd–5th rounds

7th–16th rounds

Legs (make 2)

Using yellow yarn, make a magic ring as for the head.

1st round: 2 sc into each sc. (12 sts)

3rd–8th rounds: 1 sc into each sc.

Fasten off.

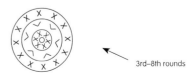

3rd–8th rounds

Feet (make 2)

Using yellow yarn, make a magic ring as for the head.

1st round: 2 sc into each sc. (12 sts)

3rd–6th rounds: 1 sc into each sc.

Fasten off.

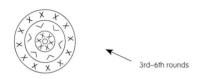

3rd–6th rounds

Hands (make 2)

Using yellow yarn, make a magic ring as for the head.

1st round: [3 hdc into next sc, 1 sc into foll sc], twice, 3 hdc into next st.

Fasten off.

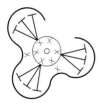

Making up

Fill the nose, neck body, tail, legs, and feet with toy stuffing. Using the photographs and the structure diagram as reference and matching yarn, stitch the nose to the head, the head to the neck, the neck to the body, and the body to the tail. Stitch the feet to the legs and the legs to the body. Using green yarn, embroider straight stitches onto the nose.

For the ears, using green yarn, join into the right side of the head. Then, working into the head stitches, work the following in a straight line toward the top of the head: 1 ch, 1 hdc into the st at base of ch, 2 dc into next st, 1 hdc into foll st, sl st into next st.

Repeat on the left side of the head but start at a stitch level with the last stitch of the first ear and work downward.

For the spine, using yellow yarn, join into the top of the tail near the tip. Then, working into the tail, body, neck, and head stitches, work the following in a straight line toward the top of the head: [4 hdc into the next sc, 1 sc into foll sc] repeat to the top of the head.

Chapter 2

Love
and
Romance

Kiss Kiss Love Birds

These feathered friends have left the flock and set up home in their very own love nest. When love birds find each other, they bond for life, so you must remember to keep this colorful couple together forever.

Size

Height: 3.1 in. (8 cm)

Materials

HOOK SIZE: C (3 mm)

YARN:

Any bright colored yarn will work equally well

Yellow or pink for head

Blue or lilac for the body and wings

Green or blue for the tummy

Pink or green for the cheeks

Yellow for the beak

OTHER MATERIALS:

Toy stuffing

2 toy safety eyes, .16 in. (4 mm)

Structure

The love birds are made in two sections: with wings and breast piece attached.

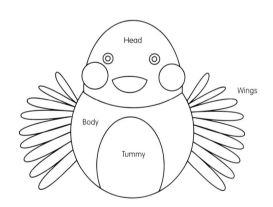

Head

Using yellow or pink yarn, make a magic ring as follows.

Make a loop with tail end of yarn on right, keeping ball end on left. Pull the ball end through loop. Make one chain through loop on hook you have drawn through to steady the circle. Work 6 sc into

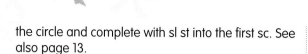

the circle and complete with sl st into the first sc. See also page 13.

1st round: 2 sc into each sc. (12 sts)

2nd round: [1 sc into next sc, 2 sc into foll 1 sc] 6 times. (18 sts)

3rd round: [1 sc into each of next 2 sc, 2 sc into foll 1 sc] 6 times. (24 sts)

4th–8th rounds: 1 sc into each sc.

Fasten off.

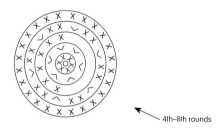

4th–8th rounds

Body

Using blue or lilac yarn, make a magic ring as for the head.

1st round: 2 sc into each sc. (12 sts)

2nd round: [1 sc into next sc, 2 sc into foll sc] 6 times. (18 sts)

3rd round: [1 sc into each of next 2 sc, 2 sc into foll sc] 6 times. (24 sts)

4th–7th rounds: 1 sc into each sc.

8th round: [1 sc into each of next 3 sc, 2 sc into foll sc] 6 times. (30 sts)

9th round: 1 sc into each sc.

10th round: [1 sc into each of next 3 sc, sc 2 tog] 6 times. (24 sts)

11th round: [1 sc into each of next 2 sc, sc 2 tog] 6 times. (18 sts)

12th–14th rounds: 1 sc into each sc.

Fasten off.

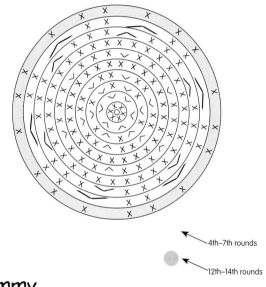

4th–7th rounds

12th–14th rounds

Tummy

Using green or blue yarn, make a magic ring as for the head.

1st round: 2 sc into each sc. (12 sts)

2nd round: [1 sc into next sc, 2 sc into foll sc] 6 times. (18 sts)

3rd round: [1 sc into each of next 2 sc, 2 sc into foll sc] 6 times. (24 sts)

4th round: [1 sc into each of next 3 sc, 2 sc into foll sc] 6 times. (30 sts)

Fasten off.

Cheeks (make 2)

Using pink or green yarn, make a magic ring as for the head.

1st round: 2 sc into each sc. (12 sts)

Fasten off.

Beak

Using yellow yarn, make a magic ring as for the head.

1st round: 2 sc into each sc. (12 sts)

2nd round: 1 sc into each sc.

Fasten off.

Wings (make 2)

Work each sc with long fur stitch loops worked as follows.

Insert the hook into the place or stitch directed, hook both sets of strands hanging down on either side of the raised index finger to create a loop, draw all the strands through the fabric, remove the index finger from the loop but hold the loop firmly against the fabric, wrap the yarn around the hook, and draw it through all the loops on the hook. Firmly pull on the loop to draw it tight.

Using blue or lilac yarn, make a magic ring as for the head.

1st round: 2 sc into each sc. (12 sts)

2nd round: [1 sc into next sc, 2 sc into foll sc] 6 times. (18 sts)

3rd round: [1 sc into each of next 2 sc, 2 sc into foll sc] 6 times. (24 sts)

4th round: [1 sc into each of next 3 sc, 2 sc into foll sc] 6 times. (30 sts)

Fasten off.

Making up

Secure the toy safety eyes approximately 4 sts apart on the sixth round and fill the head with toy stuffing. Using the photographs as reference and matching yarn, stitch the beak and cheek pieces to the head. Fill the body with toy stuffing and stitch the head, tummy, and wings in place. These little birds are forever!

Big Heart Bear

With his cute little face and cuddly charms, who could resist Big Heart Bear? He's on a mission to spread the love around. Make him for your special someone, and his or her heart will be yours forever.

Size

Height: 6.3 in. (16 cm)

Materials

HOOK SIZE: C (3 mm)

YARN:

Brown for the head, body, arms, legs, and ears

Light brown for the heart tummy

Yellow for the nose

OTHER MATERIALS:

Toy stuffing

2 toy safety eyes, .32 in. (8 mm)

Head

Using brown yarn, make a magic ring as follows.

Make a loop with tail end of yarn on right, keeping ball end on left. Pull the ball end through loop. Make one chain through loop on hook you have drawn through to steady the circle. Work 6 sc into the circle and complete with sl st into the first sc. See also page 13.

1st round: 2 sc into each sc. (12 sts)

2nd round: [1 sc into next sc, 2 sc into foll 1 sc] 6 times. (18 sts)

3rd round: [1 sc into each of next 2 sc, 2 sc into foll 1 sc] 6 times. (24 sts)

4th round: [1 sc into each of next 3 sc, 2 sc into foll sc] 6 times. (30 sts)

5th round: [1 sc into each of next 4 sc, 2 sc into foll sc] 6 times. (36 sts)

6th round: [1 sc into each of next 5 sc, 2 sc into foll sc] 6 times. (42 sts)

7th–9th rounds: 1 sc into each sc.

10th round: [1 sc into each of next 5 sc, sc 2 tog] 6 times. (36 sts)

11th round: [1 sc into each of next 4 sc, sc 2 tog] 6 times. (30 sts)

12th round: [1 sc into each of next 3 sc, sc 2 tog] 6 times. (24 sts)

13th round: [1 sc into each of next 2 sc, sc 2 tog] 6 times. (18 sts)

Secure the toy safety eyes approximately 7 sts apart on the seventh round and fill the head with toy stuffing.

14th round: [1 sc into next sc, sc 2 tog] 6 times. (12 sts)

15th round: [sc 2 tog] 6 times. (6 sts)

Fasten off.

7th–9th rounds

Body

Using brown yarn, make a magic ring as for the head.

1st round: 2 sc into each sc. (12 sts)

2nd round: [1 sc into next sc, 2 sc into foll sc] 6 times. (18 sts)

3rd round: [1 sc into each of next 2 sc, 2 sc into foll sc] 6 times. (24 sts)

4th–7th rounds: 1 sc into each sc.

8th round: [1 sc into each of next 2 sc, sc 2 tog] 6 times. (18 sts)

9th–10th rounds: 1 sc into each sc.

11th round: [1 sc into next sc, sc 2 tog] 6 times. (12 sts)

12th–13th rounds: 1 sc into each sc.

Fasten off.

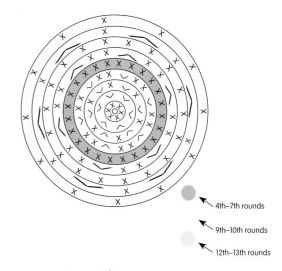

4th–7th rounds

9th–10th rounds

12th–13th rounds

Arms (make 2)

Using brown yarn, make a magic ring as for the head.

1st round: 2 sc into each sc. (12 sts)

2nd–12th rounds: 1 sc into each sc.

Fasten off.

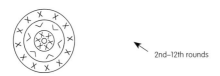

2nd–12th rounds

Legs (make 2)

Using brown yarn, make a magic ring as for the head.

Work as for legs until 9th round.

Fasten off.

Ears (make 2)

Using brown yarn, make a magic ring as for the head.

Work as for legs until 4th round.

Fasten off.

Nose

Using yellow yarn, make a magic ring as for the head.

Work as for legs until 4th round.

Fasten off.

Heart tummy

Using light brown yarn, make a magic ring as for the head.

1st round: 2 sc into each sc. (12 sts)

2nd round: 1 sc into each sc

3rd round: 1 ch, 1 sc into next sc, 3 hdc into foll 1 sc, 1 sc into each of next 2 sc, 3 hdc into next sc, 1 sc into foll sc, sl st into the next 2 sc, 1 sc into each of the next 2 sc, sl st into next 2 sc.

Fasten off.

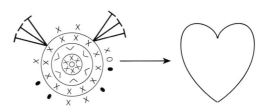

Making up

Using the photographs as reference and matching yarn, stitch the flattened ears and nose to the head.

Fill the body, arms, and legs with toy stuffing. Stitch the head, heart tummy, arms, and legs to the body. Time for the heart bear's first hug!

Wedding Joy

When the happy couple seal the knot, then it's time to get out the yarn and make this blushing bride and groom for their very own woolly wedding. Create this crocheted Mr. and Mrs., and celebrate matrimonial bliss.

Size

Bride's height: 5.5 in. (14 cm)

Materials

HOOK SIZE: C (3 mm)

YARN:

Flesh-colored for both heads and noses

Red for the cheeks

Brown for the bride's hair

White for the dress and two bows.

Gray for the top hat and groom's suit

OTHER MATERIALS:

Toy stuffing

4 toy safety eyes, .32 in. (8 mm)

5th–8th rounds

Bride's head

Using flesh-colored yarn, make a magic ring as follows.

Make a loop with tail end of yarn on right, keeping ball end on left. Pull the ball end through loop. Make one chain through loop on hook you have drawn through to steady the circle. Work 6 sc into the circle and complete with sl st into the first sc. See also page 13.

1st round: 2 sc into each sc. (12 sts)

2nd round: [1 sc into next sc, 2 sc into foll 1 sc] 6 times. (18 sts)

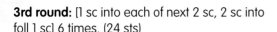

3rd round: [1 sc into each of next 2 sc, 2 sc into foll 1 sc] 6 times. (24 sts)

4th round: [1 sc into each of next 3 sc, 2 sc into foll sc] 6 times. (30 sts)

5th–8th rounds: 1 sc into each sc.

9th round: [1 sc into each of next 3 sc, sc 2 tog] 6 times. (24 sts)

10th round: [1 sc into each of next 2 sc, sc 2 tog] 6 times. (18 sts)

Secure the toy safety eyes approximately 6 sts apart on the sixth round and fill the head with toy stuffing.

11th round: [1 sc into next sc, sc 2 tog] 6 times. (12 sts)

12th round: [sc 2 tog] 6 times. (6 sts)

Fasten off.

Bride's cheeks (make 2)

Using red yarn, make a magic ring as for the bride's head.

Fasten off.

Bride's nose

Using flesh-colored yarn, make a magic ring as for the bride's head.

1st–2nd rounds: 1 sc into each sc.

Fasten off.

1st–2nd rounds

Bride's hair

4 dc-bobble = [wrap the yarn around the hook, insert the hook into fourth ch from hook, wrap yarn around hook, draw yarn through ch, wrap yarn around hook draw yarn through two loops on hook] 4 times, wrap yarn around hook draw yarn through all loops on the hook.

Using brown yarn, make 4 ch

1st row: 4 dc-bobble [4 ch, 4 dc-bobble] 27 times or as many times as you wish to curl around the bride's head.

Fasten off.

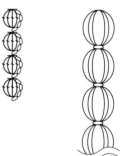

Bride's dress

Using white yarn, make a magic ring as for the bride's head.

1st round: 2 sc into each sc. (12 sts)

2nd round: [1 sc into next sc, 2 sc into foll sc] 6 times. (18 sts)

3rd round: [1 sc into each of next 2 sc, 2 sc into foll sc] 6 times. (24 sts)

4th–18th rounds: 1 sc into each sc.

Fasten off.

4th–18th rounds

Bride's dress base

Using white yarn, make a magic ring as for the bride's head.

Work as for bride's dress until 3rd round.

Fasten off.

Bride's bow

Using white, make 15 ch.

1st row: 1 hdc into the third ch from the hook, 1 hdc into each ch to end, turn. (14 sts)

2nd–4th rows: 2 ch (counts as first hdc), 1 hdc into the back loop of each hdc to end, turn.

Fasten off white yarn, join in cream.

5th–8th rows: 2 ch (counts as first hdc), 1 hdc into the back loop of each hdc to end, turn.

Fasten off.

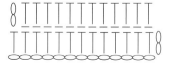

2nd–8th rows

Groom's head

Using flesh-colored yarn, make a magic ring as for the bride's head.

Work as for bride's head.

Groom's cheeks (make 2)

Using red yarn, make a magic ring as for the bride's head.

Work as for bride's cheeks.

Groom's nose

Using flesh-colored yarn, make a magic ring as for the bride's head.

Work as for groom's cheeks.

Groom's suit body

Using gray yarn, make a magic ring as for the bride's head.

1st round: 2 sc into each sc. (12 sts)

2nd round: [1 sc into next sc, 2 sc into foll sc] 6 times. (18 sts)

3rd round: [1 sc into each of next 2 sc, 2 sc into foll sc] 6 times. (24 sts)

4th round: [1 sc into each of next 3 sc, 2 sc into foll sc] 6 times. (30 sts)

5th–7th rounds: 1 sc into each sc.

8th round: [1 sc into each of next 3 sc, sc 2 tog] 6 times. (24 sts)

9th–10th rounds: 1 sc into each sc.

11th round: [1 sc into each of next 2 sc, sc 2 tog] 6 times. (18 sts)

12th–14th rounds: 1 sc into each sc.

Fasten off.

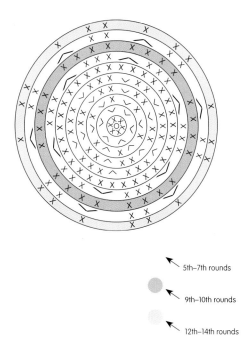

5th–7th rounds

9th–10th rounds

12th–14th rounds

Groom's legs (make 2)

Using gray yarn, make a magic ring as for the bride's head.

1st round: 2 sc into each sc. (12 sts)

2nd round: [1 sc into next sc, 2 sc into foll sc] 6 times. (18 sts)

3rd–9th rounds: 1 sc into each sc.

Fasten off.

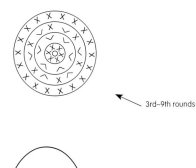

3rd–9th rounds

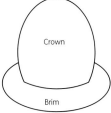

Crown

Brim

Groom's hat crown

Using gray yarn, make a magic ring as for the bride's head.

1st round: 2 sc into each sc. (12 sts)

2nd–6th rounds: 1 sc into each sc.

Fasten off.

2nd–6th rounds

Groom's hat brim

Using gray yarn, make a magic ring as for the bride's head.

1st round: 2 sc into each sc. (12 sts)

2nd round: [1 sc into next sc, 2 sc into foll sc] 6 times. (18 sts)

3rd round: [1 sc into each of next 2 sc, 2 sc into foll sc] 6 times. (24 sts)

Fasten off.

Groom's bow tie

Using white, make 8 ch.

1st row: 1 hdc into the third ch from the hook, 1 hdc into each ch to end, turn. (6 sts)

2nd–4th rows: 2 ch (counts as first hdc), 1 hdc into each sc to end, turn.

Fasten off.

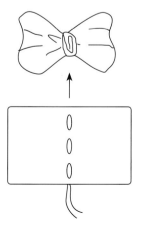

Making up

Using the photographs as reference and matching yarn, stitch the cheeks and nose to the bride's head. Starting from the center, wrap and pin the bride's hair around her head in a spiral, until it reaches ear level, then work back and forth, from side to side, in an S-shape. Stitch in place. Repeat for the groom but skip the hair instructions and, instead, stuff the hat crown, stitch it to the hat brim, and stitch both onto the groom's head.

To finish the bows: fold the bride's bow in half horizontally and stitch the top and bottom edges together; fold the groom's bow in half lengthways and stitch the selvedge edges together. Using white or cream yarn, stitch a line of running stitches around the center of the tube, pull tight and secure, wrap yarn tightly around the center of the bow, and secure.

Fill the dress with toy stuffing. Attach the bride's head and the bride's bow to the dress.

Fill the suit body and legs with toy stuffing. Attach the groom's head and legs to the suit body. Using black yarn, embroider lapel outlines onto the groom's suit. Attach the groom's bow tie to the suit.

Red Red Rose

The age of romance is not dead! If you're totally smitten, there's nothing like a single, red rose when you want to make an amorous gesture. Surprise your loved one with a tender token that will last forever.

Size

Height: 6.7 in. (17 cm)

Materials

HOOK SIZE: C (3 mm)

YARN:

Red for the rose head

Green for the leaf and stem

OTHER MATERIALS:

Craft wire, 6 in. (15 cm)

Rose head

Using red yarn, make 36 ch or a ch longer than 8 in. (20 cm) for a rose head size of your choice!

1st row: 2 dc into the fourth ch from the hook, 2 dc into each ch to end.

Fasten off.

Stem

Using green yarn, make a ch the same length as the craft wire.

Holding the wire and the chain together in the left hand (for right-handed crocheters), work the following row around the wire and encase the craft wire with double crochet stitches.

1st row: 1 sc into the second ch from the hook, 1 sc into each ch to end.

Fasten off.

Leaf

Using green yarn, make 9 ch.

1st row: 1 sc into the third ch from the hook, 1 hdc into next ch, 1 dc into each of next 2 ch, 1 hdc into foll ch, 1 sc into each of last 2 ch.

Fasten off.

Making up

Using the photographs as reference and matching yarn, roll the rose head up along its length and secure at the base with a few stitches. Stitch the leaf to the stem and the stem to the underside of the rose head.

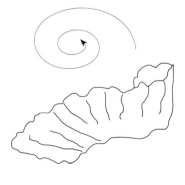

Chapter 3

Springtime is
Here!

Springtime Ducks

When cute little baby animals start to appear, it's a sure sign that spring has arrived. So when winter's over and the days start to warm up, it's time to get quacking and create your own darling duckling.

Size

Height with top tuft: 4 in. (10 cm)

Materials

HOOK SIZE: C (3 mm)

YARN:

Dark yellow for the head, body, and wings

Orange for beak

OTHER MATERIALS:

Toy stuffing

2 toy safety eyes, .32 in. (8 mm)

Structure

The Easter chick is made in two sections: with wings and a hair tuft attached.

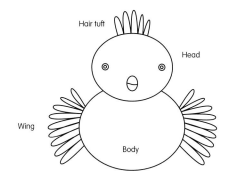

Head

Using dark yellow yarn, make a magic ring as follows.

Make a loop with tail end of yarn on right, keeping ball end on left. Pull the ball end through loop. Make one chain through loop on hook you have drawn through to steady the circle. Work 6 sc into the circle and complete with sl st into the first sc. See also page 13.

1st round: 2 sc into each sc. (12 sts)

2nd round: [1 sc into next sc, 2 sc into foll 1 sc] 6 times. (18 sts)

3rd round: [1 sc into each of next 2 sc, 2 sc into foll 1 sc] 6 times. (24 sts)

4th–8th rounds: 1 sc into each sc.

9th round: [1 sc into each of next 2 sc, sc 2 tog] 6 times. (18 sts)

Secure the toy safety eyes approximately 8 sts apart on the seventh round and fill with toy stuffing.

11th round: [1 sc into next sc, sc 2 tog] 6 times. (12 sts)

12th round: [sc 2 tog] 6 times. (6 sts)

Fasten off.

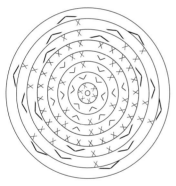

4th–8th rounds

Body

Using dark yellow yarn, make a magic ring as for the head.

1st round: 2 sc into each sc. (12 sts)

2nd round: [1 sc into next sc, 2 sc into foll sc] 6 times. (18 sts)

3rd round: [1 sc into each of next 2 sc, 2 sc into foll sc] 6 times. (24 sts)

4th round: [1 sc into each of next 3 sc, 2 sc into foll sc] 6 times. (30 sts)

5th round: [1 sc into each of next 4 sc, 2 sc into foll sc] 6 times. (36 sts)

6th round: [1 sc into each of next 5 sc, 2 sc into foll sc] 6 times. (42 sts)

7th–12th rounds: 1 sc into each sc.

13th round: [1 sc into each of next 5 sc, sc 2 tog] 6 times. (36 sts)

14th round: [1 sc into each of next 4 sc, sc 2 tog] 6 times. (30 sts)

15th round: [1 sc into each of next 3 sc, sc 2 tog] 6 times. (24 sts)

16th round: [1 sc into each of next 2 sc, sc 2 tog] 6 times. (18 sts)

17th round: [1 sc into next sc, sc 2 tog] 6 times. (12 sts)

18th round: [sc 2 tog] 6 times. (6 sts)

Fasten off.

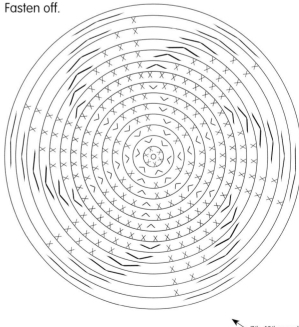

7th–12th rounds

Beak (make 2)

Using orange yarn, make 5 ch.

1st row: 1 sc into the second ch from the hook, 1 sc into each ch to end, turn. (4 sts)

2nd row: 1 ch (counts as first sc), 1 sc into each sc to end, turn.

3rd row: 1 ch (counts as first sc), sc 2 tog, 1 sc into last sc, turn.

4th row: 1 ch (counts as first sc), sc 2 tog.

Fasten off.

```
      0
    X ∧ 0
    0 X X X
    X X X X 0
    0 0 0 0
```

Wings (make 2)

Work each sc with long fur stitch loops worked as follows.

Insert the hook into the place or stitch directed, hook both sets of strands hanging down on either side of the raised index finger to create a loop, draw all the strands through the fabric, remove the index finger from the loop but hold the loop firmly against the fabric, wrap the yarn around the hook, and draw it through all the loops on the hook. Firmly pull on the loop to draw it tight.

Using double stranded dark yellow yarn, make a magic ring as for the head.

1st round: 2 sc into each sc. (12 sts)

2nd round: [1 sc into next sc, 2 sc into foll sc] 6 times. (18 sts)

3rd round: [1 sc into each of next 2 sc, 2 sc into foll sc] 6 times. (24 sts)

4th round: [1 sc into each of next 3 sc, 2 sc into foll sc] 6 times. (30 sts)

Fasten off.

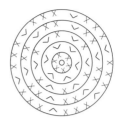

Hair tuft

Work each sc with long fur stitch loops worked as above for the wings.

Using double stranded dark yellow yarn, make a magic ring as for the head.

1st round: 2 sc into each sc. (12 sts)

Fasten off.

Making up

Using the photographs as reference and matching yarn, stitch the beak pieces to the face and the hair tuft to the head.

Fill the body with toy stuffing. To create the flattened shape of the body, secure a length of yarn to the center of the base, stitch through the depth of the body, pull tight, and secure the shape with a stitch. Stitch the head and wings to the body. Isn't it tweet?

Dancing Daffodils

You know that spring has truly sprung when beautiful blooms start bursting out all over. Sunshine yellow and full of joy, these dancing daffodils are set to brighten up any day.

Size

Height: 6.7 in. (17 cm)

Materials

HOOK SIZE: C (3 mm)

YARN:

Cream or yellow for the petals

Yellow or orange for the flower center

Green for the stem

OTHER MATERIALS:

Craft wire, 6 in. (15 cm)

Petal (make 6)

Using cream or yellow yarn, make 7 ch.

1st row: 1 sc into the second ch from the hook, 1 sc into each ch to end. (6 sts)

2nd–3rd rows: 1 ch, 1 sc into each sc to end.

4th row: 1 ch, 1 sc into next sc, [sc 2 tog] twice, 1 sc into next sc. (4 sts)

5th row: 1 ch, 1 sc into each sc to end.

6th row: 1 ch, 1 sc into next sc, sc 2 tog, 1 sc into next sc. (3 sts)

7th row: 1 ch, sc 2 tog.

Fasten off.

Flower center

Using yellow or orange yarn, make a magic ring as follows.

Make a loop with tail end of yarn on right, keeping ball end on left. Pull the ball end through loop. Make one chain through loop on hook you have drawn through to steady the circle. Work 6 sc into the circle and complete with sl st into the first sc. See also page 13.

1st round: 2 sc into each sc. (12 sts)

2nd–5th rounds: 1 sc into each sc.

Fasten off.

2nd–5th rounds

Stem

Using green yarn, make a magic ring as for the flower center.

Work 1 sc into each sc until the piece measures 6 in. (15 cm).

Fasten off.

6 in. (15 cm)

Making up

Using the photographs as reference and matching yarn, stitch the flower petals to the flower center. Make a small loop at either end of the craft wire, slide the craft wire into the center of the stem, and stitch through the wire loops to secure it in place. Stitch the stem to the underside of the flower head.

You have just made it!

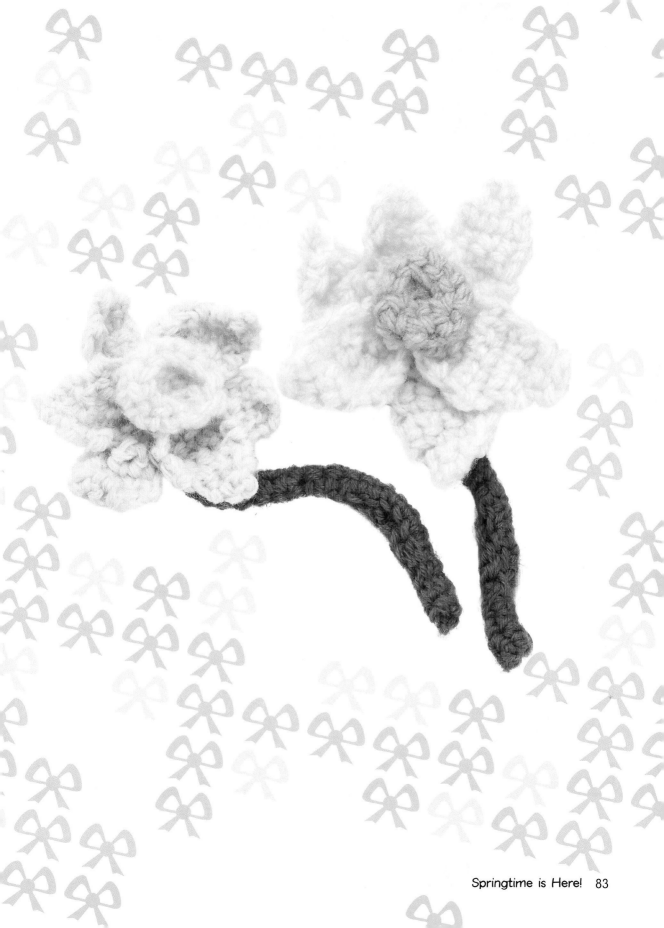

Eggs in Basket

If you want a really egg-citing gift for an eggs-tra special friend, then why not make them happy with a jolly striped egg? Make half a dozen of them and you can put all your eggs in one basket whenever you want.

Size

Length: 2.4 in. (6 cm)

Materials

HOOK SIZE: C (3 mm)

YARN:

Any yarn or color

OTHER MATERIALS:

Toy stuffing

Using yarn of your choice, make a magic ring as follows.

Make a loop with tail end of yarn on right, keeping ball end on left. Pull the ball end through loop. Make one chain through loop on hook you have drawn through to steady the circle. Work 6 sc into the circle and complete with sl st into the first sc. See also page 13.

1st round: 2 sc into each sc. (12 sts)

2nd round: [1 sc into next sc, 2 sc into foll 1 sc] 6 times. (18 sts)

3rd round: [1 sc into each of next 2 sc, 2 sc into foll 1 sc] 6 times. (24 sts)

4th–11th rounds: 1 sc into each sc.

12th round: [1 sc into each of next 2 sc, sc 2 tog] 6 times. (18 sts)

Fill the egg with toy stuffing.

13th round: [1 sc into next sc, sc 2 tog] 6 times. (12 sts)

14th round: [sc 2 tog] 6 times. (6 sts)

Fasten off.

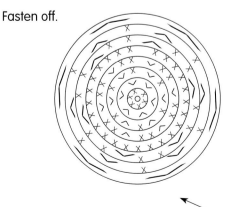

4th–11th rounds

Using different yarns and embroidery stitches, design your own eggs, and then have fun, hiding them for others to find!

Hop Hop Easter Bunny!

At Easter time, this bouncy bunny is bound to bring a super-sweet surprise or two, but you have to find them first! If you give him a big cuddle, maybe he'll tell you where all the chocolate is hidden.

Size

Height: 6.7 in. (17 cm)

Materials

HOOK SIZE: C (3 mm)

YARN:

White for the head, body, arms, legs, feet, tail, ears, and nose

Pink for the cheeks

Brown for the embroider of the mouth

OTHER MATERIALS:

Toy stuffing

2 black beads, .16 in. (4 mm)

Head

Using white yarn, make a magic ring as follows.

Make a loop with tail end of yarn on right, keeping ball end on left. Pull the ball end through loop. Make one chain through loop on hook you have drawn through to steady the circle. Work 6 sc into the circle and complete with sl st into the first sc. See also page 13.

1st round: 2 sc into each sc. (12 sts)

2nd round: [1 sc into next sc, 2 sc into foll 1 sc] 6 times. (18 sts)

3rd round: [1 sc into each of next 2 sc, 2 sc into foll 1 sc] 6 times. (24 sts)

4th round: [1 sc into each of next 3 sc, 2 sc into foll 1 sc] 6 times. (30 sts)

5th–10th rounds: 1 sc into each sc.

11th round: [1 sc into each of next 3 sc, sc 2 tog] 6 times. (24 sts)

12th round: [1 sc into each of next 2 sc, sc 2 tog] 6 times. (18 sts)

Secure the toy safety eyes approximately 6 sts apart on the eighth round and fill with toy stuffing.

13th round: [1 sc into next sc, sc 2 tog] 6 times. (12 sts)

14th round: [sc 2 tog] 6 times. (6 sts)

Fasten off.

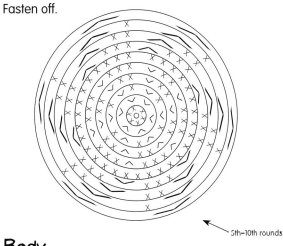

5th–10th rounds

Body

Using white yarn, make a magic ring as for the head.

1st round: 2 sc into each sc. (12 sts)

2nd round: [1 sc into next sc, 2 sc into foll sc] 6 times. (18 sts)

3rd round: [1 sc into each of next 2 sc, 2 sc into foll sc] 6 times. (24 sts)

4th round: [1 sc into each of next 3 sc, 2 sc into foll sc] 6 times. (30 sts)

5th–10th rounds: 1 sc into each sc.

11th round: [1 sc into each of next 3 sc, sc 2 tog] 6 times. (24 sts)

12th round: [1 sc into each of next 2 sc, sc 2 tog] 6 times. (18 sts)

13th–14th rounds: 1 sc into each sc.

Fill the body with toy stuffing.

15th round: [1 sc into next sc, sc 2 tog] 6 times. (12 sts)

16th–17th rounds: 1 sc into each sc.

Fasten off.

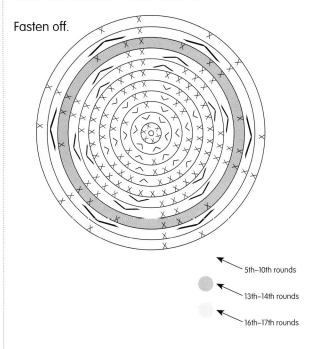

5th–10th rounds

13th–14th rounds

16th–17th rounds

Cheeks (make 2)

Using pink yarn, make a magic ring as for the head.

1st round: 2 sc into each sc. (12 sts)

2nd–3rd rounds: 1 sc into each sc.

Fasten off.

2nd–3rd rounds

Nose and Tail

Using white yarn, make a magic ring as for the head.

Work one piece for each as for cheeks.

Ears (make 2)

Using white yarn, make a magic ring as for the head.

1st round: 2 sc into each sc. (12 sts)

2nd–12th rounds: 1 sc into each sc.

Fasten off.

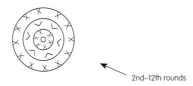

2nd–12th rounds

Legs (make 2)

Using white yarn, make a magic ring as for the head.

1st round: 2 sc into each sc. (12 sts)

2nd round: [1 sc into next sc, 2 sc into foll sc] 6 times. (18 sts)

3rd–6th rounds: 1 sc into each sc.

Fasten off.

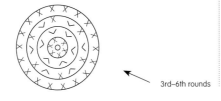

3rd–6th rounds

Feet (make 2)

Using white yarn, make a magic ring as for the head.

1st round: 2 sc into each sc. (12 sts)

2nd–4th rounds: 1 sc into each sc.

Fasten off.

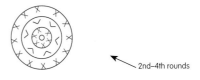

2nd–4th rounds

Arms (make 2)

Using white yarn, make a magic ring as for the head.

1st round: 2 sc into each sc. (12 sts)

2nd–6th rounds: 1 sc into each sc.

Fasten off.

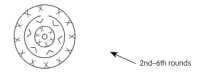

2nd–6th rounds

Making up

Using the photographs as reference and matching yarn, stitch the flattened ears, cheeks and nose to the head. Using brown yarn, embroider the nose.

Fill the body and legs with toy stuffing. Do not stuff the arms and feet. Stitch the head to the body, the arms on the front of the body, and the legs to the side of the body. Stitch the feet to the legs and the tail to the back of the body. With a twitch of the nose, your bunny is ready to hop off!

Chapter 4
Party Time!

Party Animal

When you're planning the perfect party, don't forget an invite for this perky little panda. There's nothing he likes more than a good shindig, so make sure he's on the guest list if you want things to go with a bang.

Size

Height: 6.3 in. (16 cm)

Materials

HOOK SIZE: C (3 mm)

YARN:

White for the head and nose

Brown for the ears, eye patches, nose, arms and legs

Pink for the hat

Bright green for the hat decoration

OTHER MATERIALS:

Toy stuffing

2 toy safety eyes, .32 in. (8 mm)

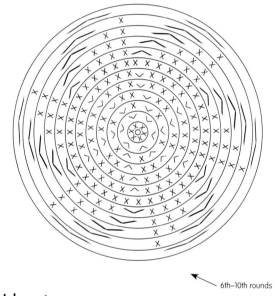

6th–10th rounds

Head

Using brown yarn, make a magic ring as follows.

Make a loop with tail end of yarn on right, keeping ball end on left. Pull the ball end through loop. Make one chain through loop on hook you have drawn through to steady the circle. Work 6 sc into the circle and complete with sl st into the first sc. See also page 13.

1st round: 2 sc into each sc. (12 sts)

2nd round: [1 sc into next sc, 2 sc into foll 1 sc] 6 times. (18 sts)

3rd round: [1 sc into each of next 2 sc, 2 sc into foll 1 sc] 6 times. (24 sts)

4th round: [1 sc into each of next 3 sc, 2 sc into foll 1 sc] 6 times. (30 sts)

5th round: [1 sc into each of next 4 sc, 2 sc into foll 1 sc] 6 times. (36 sts)

6th–10th rounds: 1 sc into each sc.

11th round: [1 sc into each of next 4 sc, sc 2 tog] 6 times. (30 sts)

12th round: [1 sc into each of next 3 sc, sc 2 tog] 6 times. (24 sts)

13th round: [1 sc into each of next 2 sc, sc 2 tog] 6 times. (18 sts)

Fill the head with toy stuffing.

14th round: [1 sc into next sc, sc 2 tog] 6 times. (12 sts)

15th round: [sc 2 tog] 6 times. (6 sts)

Fasten off.

Body

Using white yarn, make a magic ring as for the head.

1st round: 2 sc into each sc. (12 sts)

2nd round: [1 sc into next sc, 2 sc into foll sc] 6 times. (18 sts)

3rd round: [1 sc into each of next 2 sc, 2 sc into foll sc] 6 times. (24 sts)

4th–5th rounds: 1 sc into each sc.

6th round: [1 sc into each of next 2 sc, sc 2 tog] 6 times. (18 sts)

7th–14th rounds: 1 sc into each sc.

Fasten off.

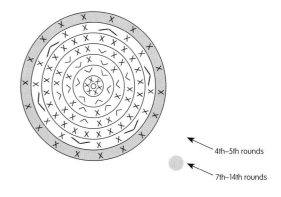

4th–5th rounds

7th–14th rounds

Legs (make 2)

Using brown yarn, make a magic ring as for the head.

1st round: 2 sc into each sc. (12 sts)

2nd–8th rounds: 1 sc into each sc.

Fasten off.

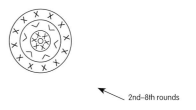

2nd–8th rounds

Arms (make 2)

Using brown yarn, make a magic ring as for the head.

Work as for legs.

Eye patches (make 2)

Using brown yarn, make a magic ring as for the head.

1st round: 2 sc into each sc. (12 sts)

Fasten off.

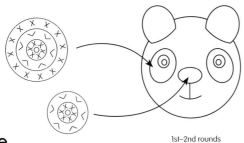

1st–2nd rounds

Nose

Using brown yarn, make a magic ring as for the head.

1st–2nd rounds: 1 sc into each sc.

Fasten off.

Ears (make 2)

Using brown yarn, make a magic ring as for the head.

1st round: 2 sc into each sc. (12 sts)

2nd–4th rounds: 1 sc into each sc.

Fasten off.

2nd–4th rounds

Hat

Using pink yarn, make a magic ring as for the head.

1st–2nd rounds: 1 sc into each sc.

3rd round: 2 sc into each sc. (12 sts)

4th–5th rounds: 1 sc into each sc.

6th round: [1 sc into next sc, 2 sc into foll sc] 6 times. (18 sts)

7th–8th rounds: 1 sc into each sc.

Fasten off.

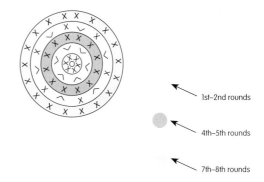

1st–2nd rounds

4th–5th rounds

7th–8th rounds

Making up

Fill the head, body, legs, arms, and hat with toy stuffing.

Attach the toy safety eyes to the eye patches.

Using the photographs as reference and matching yarn, stitch the nose, eyes, and flattened ears to the head and the head to the body. Stitch the legs and arms to the body.

Using brown yarn, embroider straight stitches for the mouth. Using green yarn, embroider straight stitch blocks on to the hat. And, then, at a jaunty angle, put the hat on him: joy!

Special Gifts

We all love a beautifully wrapped present, so why not make the gift wrap the gift? Make these beribboned little boxes to mark any memorable occasion, and you can be certain of spreading a little happiness.

Size

Height: 2.7 in. (7 cm)

Width: 2.7 in. (7 cm)

Materials

HOOK SIZE: C (3 mm)

YARN:

Green or pink

OTHER MATERIALS:

Toy stuffing

Cardboard

Ribbon, 12 in. (30 cm)

Structure

The finished box piece should resemble a T-shape. The area indicated in the center of the top bar of the T-shape becomes the bottom of the box, and the sections of fabric surrounding it are folded upward along the dashed line. The vertical bar of the T-shape is folded around the remaining sides of the box.

Box

Using green or pink yarn, make a 37 ch.

1st row: 1 sc into the third ch from the hook, 1 sc into each of next 35 ch, turn. (36 sts)

2nd–12th rows: 1 ch (counts as first sc), 1 sc into each sc, turn.

Fasten off.

Rejoin yarn to 13th st from edge.

13th row: 1 ch (counts as first sc), 1 sc into next 11 sts, turn. (12 sts)

14th–48th rows: 1 ch (counts as first sc), 1 sc into each sc, turn.

Fasten off.

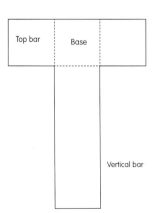

```
XXXXXXXXXXX0
0XXXXXXXXXX
XXXXXXXXXXX0
0XXXXXXXXXX
XXXXXXXXXXX0
0XXXXXXXXXX
XXXXXXXXXXX0
0XXXXXXXXXX
XXXXXXXXXXX0
0XXXXXXXXXX
XXXXXXXXXXX0
0XXXXXXXXXX
XXXXXXXXXXX0
0XXXXXXXXXX
XXXXXXXXXXX0
0XXXXXXXXXX
XXXXXXXXXXX0
0XXXXXXXXXX
XXXXXXXXXXX0
0XXXXXXXXXX
XXXXXXXXXXX0
0XXXXXXXXXX
XXXXXXXXXXX0
0XXXXXXXXXX
XXXXXXXXXXX0
0XXXXXXXXXX
XXXXXXXXXXX0
0XXXXXXXXXX
XXXXXXXXXXX0
0XXXXXXXXXX
XXXXXXXXXXX0
XXXXXXXXXXXXXXXXXXXXXXXXXXXXXXXXX0
0XXXXXXXXXXXXXXXXXXXXXXXXXXXXXXXXX
XXXXXXXXXXXXXXXXXXXXXXXXXXXXXXXXX0
0XXXXXXXXXXXXXXXXXXXXXXXXXXXXXXXXX
XXXXXXXXXXXXXXXXXXXXXXXXXXXXXXXXX0
0XXXXXXXXXXXXXXXXXXXXXXXXXXXXXXXXX
XXXXXXXXXXXXXXXXXXXXXXXXXXXXXXXXX0
0XXXXXXXXXXXXXXXXXXXXXXXXXXXXXXXXX
XXXXXXXXXXXXXXXXXXXXXXXXXXXXXXXXX0
0XXXXXXXXXXXXXXXXXXXXXXXXXXXXXXXXX
XXXXXXXXXXXXXXXXXXXXXXXXXXXXXXXXX0
0000000000000000000000000000000000
```

Making up

Using the photographs as reference and matching yarn, fold as indicated on structure diagram. Pin and stitch edges, leaving one edge open. If you want to stiffen the box slightly, cut out four squares of cardboard to fit each side of the cube, and slip these into the box so each rests against one side of the box. Stuff the box to hold the cardboard in place and stitch the opening closed. To finish, tie a length of ribbon around the box.

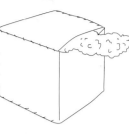

Happy Birthday Cake

No need to cut the cake or blow out the candles on this super birthday surprise. Create this creamy, crochet confection, and you will have a real treat that keeps for every anniversary party.

Size

Height: 8 in. (20 cm)

Materials

HOOK SIZE: C (3 mm)

YARN:

White for the cakes

Cream for the candle

Pink for the candle

Brown for the chocolate decoration

Red for the cherries and flame

OTHER MATERIALS:

Toy stuffing

Cardboard

Structure

The birthday cake is made in two tiers using three pieces: bottom tier, bottom tier base, and top tier.

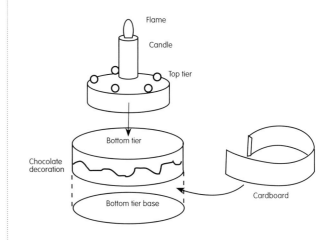

8th–14th rounds

Bottom tier

Using white yarn, make a magic ring as follows.

Make a loop with tail end of yarn on right, keeping ball end on left. Pull the ball end through loop. Make one chain through loop on hook you have drawn through to steady the circle. Work 6 sc into the circle and complete with sl st into the first sc. See also page 13.

1st round: 2 sc into each sc. (12 sts)

2nd round: [1 sc into next sc, 2 sc into foll 1 sc] 6 times. (18 sts)

3rd round: [1 sc into each of next 2 sc, 2 sc into foll 1 sc] 6 times. (24 sts)

4th round: [1 sc into each of next 3 sc, 2 sc into foll sc] 6 times. (30 sts)

5th round: [1 sc into each of next 4 sc, 2 sc into foll sc] 6 times. (36 sts)

6th round: [1 sc into each of next 5 sc, 2 sc into foll sc] 6 times. (42 sts)

7th round: [1 sc into each of next 6 sc, 2 sc into foll sc] 6 times. (48 sts)

8th–14th rounds: 1 sc into each sc.

Fasten off.

Bottom tier base

Using white yarn, make a magic ring as for the bottom tier.

1st round: 2 sc into each sc. (12 sts)

2nd round: [1 sc into next sc, 2 sc into foll 1 sc] 6 times. (18 sts)

3rd round: [1 sc into each of next 2 sc, 2 sc into foll 1 sc] 6 times. (24 sts)

4th round: [1 sc into each of next 3 sc, 2 sc into foll sc] 6 times. (30 sts)

5th round: [1 sc into each of next 4 sc, 2 sc into foll sc] 6 times. (36 sts)

6th round: [1 sc into each of next 5 sc, 2 sc into foll sc] 6 times. (42 sts)

7th round: [1 sc into each of next 6 sc, 2 sc into foll sc] 6 times. (48 sts)

Fasten off.

Top tier

Using white yarn, make a magic ring as for the bottom tier.

1st round: 2 sc into each sc. (12 sts)

2nd round: [1 sc into next sc, 2 sc into foll 1 sc] 6 times. (18 sts)

3rd round: [1 sc into each of next 2 sc, 2 sc into foll 1 sc] 6 times. (24 sts)

4th round: [1 sc into each of next 3 sc, 2 sc into foll sc] 6 times. (30 sts)

5th round: [1 sc into each of next 4 sc, 2 sc into foll sc] 6 times. (36 sts)

6th–12th rounds: 1 sc into each sc.

Fasten off.

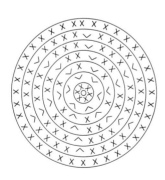

6th–12th rounds

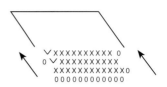

Candle

Using cream yarn, make 13 ch.

1st row: 1 sc into the second ch from the hook, 1 sc into each ch, turn.

2nd row: 1 ch, 2 sc into first st, 1 sc into each of next 10 sc, turn.

Join in pink yarn.

3rd row: 1 ch, skip 1 sc, 1 sc into each of next 10 sc, 2 sc into the last st, turn.

4th row: 1 ch, 2 sc into first st, 1 sc into each of next 10 sc, turn.

5th row: Using cream yarn, 1 ch, skip 1 sc, 1 sc into each of next 10 sc, 2 sc into the last st, turn.

6th row: 1 ch, 2 sc into first st, 1 sc into each of next 10 sc, turn.

Repeat the last 4 rows twice more.

Repeat 3rd–4th rows once more.

Fasten off.

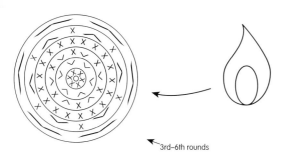

3rd–6th rounds

Flame

Using red yarn, make a magic ring as for the bottom tier.

1st round: 2 sc into each sc. (12 sts)

2nd round: [1 sc into next sc, 2 sc into foll 1 sc] 6 times. (18 sts)

3rd–6th rounds: 1 sc into each sc.

7th round: [1 sc into next sc, sc 2 tog] 6 times. (12 sts)

8th round: [sc 2 tog] 6 times. (6 sts)

Fasten off.

Chocolate decoration

4 dc-bobble = [wrap the yarn around the hook, insert the hook into fourth ch from hook, wrap yarn around hook, draw yarn through ch, wrap yarn around hook draw yarn through two loops on hook] 4 times, wrap yarn around hook draw yarn through all loops on the hook.

Using brown yarn, make 4 ch.

1st row: 4 dc-bobble [4 ch, 4 dc-bobble] 30 times or as many times as you wish to wrap around the bottom tier.

Fasten off.

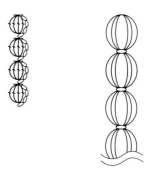

Cherries (make 5)

Using red yarn, make a magic ring as for the bottom tier.

1st round: 2 sc into each sc. (12 sts)

2nd–5th rounds: 1 sc into each sc.

Fasten off and use the yarn tail to gather the edge.

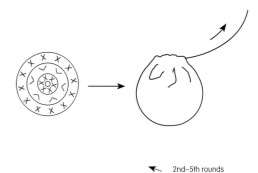

2nd–5th rounds

Making up

Cut a length of cardboard equal to the circumference of the bottom tier. Position the cardboard inside the bottom tier against the sides and hold in place with toy stuffing. Stitch the base to the bottom tier. Pin the top tier to the bottom tier, partially stitch in place, fill the top tier with toy stuffing, and complete the seam.

Stitch the edge of the first row and the edge of the last row of the candle together. Cut the cardboard to match the length of the candle and roll it into a cylinder shape. Place the cardboard roll and toy stuffing into the candle body. Gather the top edge and secure. Stitch the flame in place.

Using the photographs as reference and matching yarn, stitch the candle and the cherries to the top tier, and the chocolate decoration to the bottom tier.

This is one candle no one will be able to blow out!

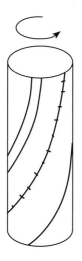

Hooray Bubbles!

When there's something to celebrate—whatever the occasion—it's time to break out the bubbles. So have some fun with the fizz, and see if you can pop the cork on this charming champagne surprise.

Size

Height: 10 in. (25 cm)

Materials

HOOK SIZE: C (3 mm)

YARN:

Green for the bottle

White for the label

Brown for the ribbon

Red for the seal

Gold Lurex or sparkly yarn for the foil

Yellow for the foil

OTHER MATERIALS:

Toy stuffing

Structure

Champagne bottle is made with five sections.

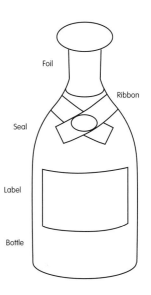

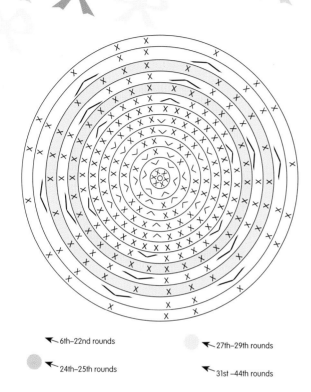

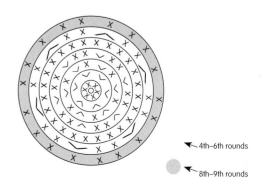

←— 6th–22nd rounds

←— 24th–25th rounds

←— 27th–29th rounds

←— 31st –44th rounds

Bottle

Using green yarn, make a magic ring as follows.

Make a loop with tail end of yarn on right, keeping ball end on left. Pull the ball end through loop. Make one chain through loop on hook you have drawn through to steady the circle. Work 6 sc into the circle and complete with sl st into the first sc. See also page 13.

1st round: 2 sc into each sc. (12 sts)

2nd round: [1 sc into next sc, 2 sc into foll 1 sc] 6 times. (18 sts)

3rd round: [1 sc into each of next 2 sc, 2 sc into foll 1 sc] 6 times. (24 sts)

4th round: [1 sc into each of next 3 sc, 2 sc into foll sc] 6 times. (30 sts)

5th round: [1 sc into each of next 4 sc, 2 sc into foll sc] 6 times. (36 sts)

6th–22nd rounds: 1 sc into each sc.

23rd round: [1 sc into each of next 4 sc, sc 2 tog] 6 times. (30 sts)

24th–25th rounds: 1 sc into each sc.

26th round: [1 sc into each of next 3 sc, sc 2 tog] 6 times. (24 sts)

27th–28th rounds: 1 sc into each sc.

Fasten off green yarn, and join in yellow and gold Lurex double stranded.

29th round: 1 sc into each sc.

30th round: [1 sc into each of next 2 sc, sc 2 tog] 6 times. (18 sts)

31st–44th rounds: 1 sc into each sc.

Fasten off.

Foil

Using yellow and gold Lurex yarn stranded together, make a magic ring as for the bottle.

←— 4th–6th rounds

←— 8th–9th rounds

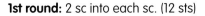

1st round: 2 sc into each sc. (12 sts)

2nd round: [1 sc into next sc, 2 sc into foll sc] 6 times. (18 sts)

3rd round: [1 sc into each of next 2 sc, 2 sc into foll sc] 6 times. (24 sts)

4th–6th rounds: 1 sc into each sc.

7th round: [1 sc into each of next 2 sc, sc 2 tog] 6 times. (18 sts)

8th–9th rounds: 1 sc into each sc.

Fasten off.

Ribbon

Using brown yarn, make 8 ch.

1st row: 1 hdc into the third ch from the hook, 1 hdc into each ch, turn. (6 sts)

2nd row: 2 ch (counts as first hdc), 1 hdc into the back loop of each sc, turn.

Repeat the last row until the ribbon is long enough to go around the neck of the bottle.

Seal

Using red yarn, make a magic ring as for the bottle.

1st round: 2 sc into each sc. (12 sts)

2nd round: [1 sc into next sc, 2 sc into foll sc] 6 times. (18 sts)

Fasten off.

Label

Using brown yarn, make 18 ch.

1st row: 1 hdc into the third ch from the hook, 1 hdc into each ch, turn. (16 sts)

2nd–7th rows: 2 ch (counts as first hdc), 1 hdc into the back loop of each sc, turn.

Making up

Using the structure diagram and photographs as reference, stuff and assemble the bottle and foil pieces. Stitch the ribbon, seal, and label in place, and perhaps embroider a name onto the label for a champagne shower of appreciation!

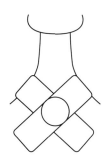

Time to Party!

When the long, hot days of summer arrive, it's time to get out in the backyard and bring out the grill. So whip up a quick crocheted kebab and a corn-on-the-cob to celebrate while the sun shines.

Size

Ear of corn length: 2.4 in. (6 cm)

Onion width: 2.7 in. (7 cm)

Meat chunk and tomato width: 2.3 in. (6 cm)

Pepper length: 2.6 in. (6.5 cm)

Materials

HOOK SIZE: C (3 mm)

YARN:

Yellow and cream for the ear of corn

Cream and brown for the onion

Brown for the meat

Red for the tomato

Green for the pepper

OTHER MATERIALS:

Toy stuffing

Wooden skewer

Structure of ear of corn

Sweet corn is made of the corn and two cob end pieces.

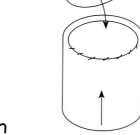

Corn

Using yellow yarn, make a magic ring as follows.

Make a loop with tail end of yarn on right, keeping ball end on left. Pull the ball end through loop. Make one chain through loop on hook you have drawn through to steady the circle. Work 6 sc into the circle and complete with sl st into the first sc. See also page 13.

1st round: 2 sc into each sc. (12 sts)

2nd round: [1 sc into next sc, 2 sc into foll 1 sc] 6 times. (18 sts)

3rd round: [1 sc into each of next 2 sc, 2 sc into foll 1 sc] 6 times. (24 sts)

4th round: [1 sc into each of next 3 sc, 2 sc into foll sc] 6 times. (30 sts)

5th–12th rounds: 1 sc into each sc.

13th round: [1 sc into each of next 3 sc, sc 2 tog] 6 times. (24 sts)

14th round: [1 sc into each of next 2 sc, sc 2 tog] 6 times. (18 sts)

Fill the corn with toy stuffing.

15th round: [1 sc into next sc, sc 2 tog] 6 times. (12 sts)

16th round: [sc 2 tog] 6 times. (6 sts)

Fasten off.

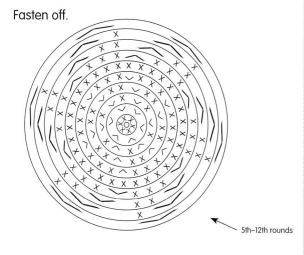

5th–12th rounds

Cob end (make 2)

Using cream yarn, make a magic ring as for the corn.

Work as for legs until 3rd round.

Fasten off.

Making up

Using the structure diagram and photographs as reference, assemble the corn and cob end pieces.

Onion

Using cream yarn, make a magic ring as for the corn.

1st round: 2 sc into each sc. (12 sts)

2nd round: [1 sc into next sc, 2 sc into foll 1 sc] 6 times. (18 sts)

3rd round: [1 sc into each of next 2 sc, 2 sc into foll 1 sc] 6 times. (24 sts)

4th round: [1 sc into each of next 3 sc, 2 sc into foll sc] 6 times. (30 sts)

Fasten off.

Making up

Using the photographs as reference, fold the circle in half, and using brown yarn, embroider concentric lines of straight stitches.

Tomato

Using red yarn, make a magic ring as for the corn.

Work as for the onion.

Using the photographs as reference, fold the circle in half and stitch the edges.

Meat

Using brown yarn, make a magic ring as for the corn.

1st round: 2 sc into each sc. (12 sts)

2nd round: [1 sc into next sc, 2 sc into foll 1 sc] 6 times. (18 sts)

3rd round: [1 sc into each of next 2 sc, 2 sc into foll 1 sc] 6 times. (24 sts)

4th round: [1 sc into each of next 3 sc, 2 sc into foll sc] 6 times. (30 sts)

5th–12th rounds: 1 sc into each sc.

Fasten off.

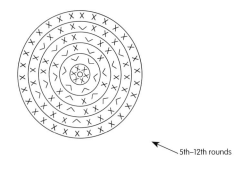

5th–12th rounds

Making up

Using the photographs as reference, flatten the cylinder, and using brown yarn, embroider random long parallel straight stitches to make it look like well-grilled meat!

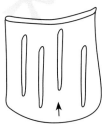

Green pepper

Using green yarn, make 16 ch.

1st row: 1 sc into the second ch from the hook, 1 sc into each ch to end. (15 sts)

2nd–5th rows: 1 ch, 1 sc into the back loop of each sc.

Fasten off.

Making up

Using the photographs as reference, fold the rectangle in half lengthways and stitch neighboring short edges together.

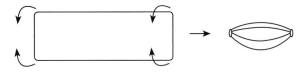

Finishing

Place all the yummy vegetables and meat onto a wooden skewer.

Chapter 5
Congratulations!

Oh So Clever!

If one of your friends or family is a real intellectual, then be sure to reward his or her academic achievement. So when it's time to dish out the diplomas, celebrate exam success with this wise little owl.

Size

Height: 5 in. (12.5 cm)

Materials

HOOK SIZE: C (3 mm)

YARN:

Pale brown for the head, body, and ears

White and pale blue for the eyes

Yellow for the beak

Purple mohair for the tummy

Black for the hat

OTHER MATERIALS:

Toy stuffing

2 mismatched toy safety eyes, .32 in. (8 mm)

Structure

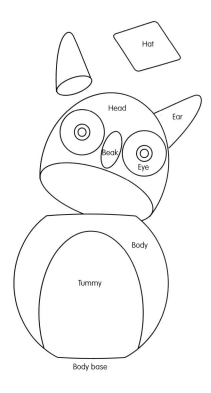

Head

Using pale brown yarn, make a magic ring as follows.

Make a loop with tail end of yarn on right, keeping ball end on left. Pull the ball end through loop. Make one chain through loop on hook you have drawn through to steady the circle. Work 6 sc into the circle and complete with sl st into the first sc. See also page 13.

1st round: 2 sc into each sc. (12 sts)

2nd round: [1 sc into next sc, 2 sc into foll 1 sc] 6 times. (18 sts)

3rd round: [1 sc into each of next 2 sc, 2 sc into foll 1 sc] 6 times. (24 sts)

4th round: [1 sc into each of next 3 sc, 2 sc into foll sc] 6 times. (30 sts)

5th round: [1 sc into each of next 4 sc, 2 sc into foll sc] 6 times. (36 sts)

6th–15th rounds: 1 sc into each sc.

Fasten off.

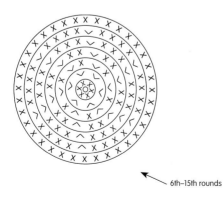

6th–15th rounds

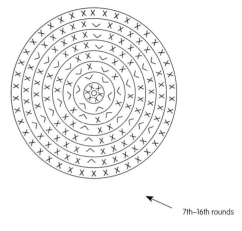

7th–16th rounds

Body

Using pale brown yarn, make a magic ring as for the head.

1st round: 2 sc into each sc. (12 sts)

2nd round: [1 sc into next sc, 2 sc into foll sc] 6 times. (18 sts)

3rd round: [1 sc into each of next 2 sc, 2 sc into foll sc] 6 times. (24 sts)

4th round: [1 sc into each of next 3 sc, 2 sc into foll sc] 6 times. (30 sts)

5th round: [1 sc into each of next 4 sc, 2 sc into foll sc] 6 times. (36 sts)

6th round: [1 sc into each of next 5 sc, 2 sc into foll sc] 6 times. (42 sts)

7th–16th rounds: 1 sc into each sc.

Fasten off.

Eyes (make 2)

Using white yarn, make a magic ring as for the head.

Fasten off white yarn, and join in pale blue yarn.

1st round: 2 sc into each sc. (12 sts)

2nd round: [1 sc into next sc, 2 sc into foll sc] 6 times. (18 sts)

Fasten off.

Ears (make 2)

Using pale brown yarn, make a magic ring as for the head.

1st–2nd rounds: 1 sc into each sc. (6 sts)

3rd round: 2 sc into each sc. (12 sts)

4th round: [1 sc into next sc, 2 sc into foll sc] 6 times. (18 sts)

5th–7th rounds: 1 sc into each sc.

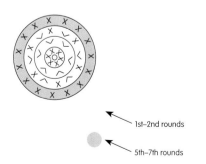

1st–2nd rounds

5th–7th rounds

Tummy

Using purple mohair yarn, make a magic ring as for the head.

1st round: 2 sc into each sc. (12 sts)

2nd round: [1 sc into next sc, 2 sc into foll sc] 6 times. (18 sts)

3rd round: [1 sc into each of next 2 sc, 2 sc into foll sc] 6 times. (24 sts)

4th round: [1 sc into each of next 3 sc, 2 sc into foll sc] 6 times. (30 sts)

5th round: [1 sc into each of next 4 sc, 2 sc into foll sc] 6 times. (36 sts)

Fasten off.

Beak

Using yellow yarn, make 7 ch.

1st row: 1 sc into the second ch from the hook, 1 sc into each ch to end, turn. (6 sts)

2nd row: 1 ch, skip the st at the base of the ch, 1 sc into each of next 5 sc turn. (5 sts)

3rd row: 1 ch, skip the st at the base of the ch, 1 sc into each of next 4 sc, turn. (4 sts)

4th row: 1 ch, skip the st at the base of the ch, 1 sc into each of next 3 sc, turn. (3 sts)

5th row: 1 ch, skip the st at the base of the ch, 1 sc into each of next 2 sc, turn. (2 sts)

6th row: 1 ch, skip the st at the base of the ch, 1 sc into next 1 sc, turn. (1 st)

Fasten off.

```
    0 ×
    × × 0
  0 × × ×
  × × × × 0
0 × × × × ×
× × × × × × 0
○○○○○○○
```

Fold the beak in half along the chain edge and stitch the selvedge edges together.

Hat

Using black yarn, make 8 ch.

1st row: 1 hdc into the third ch from the hook (counts as first hdc), 1 hdc into each ch to end, turn. (7 sts)

2nd row: 2 ch, 1 hdc into each of next 6 sc, turn.

Repeat the last row until the length measures twice the width.

```
T T T T T T 8
8 T T T T T T
T T T T T T 8
○○○○○○
```

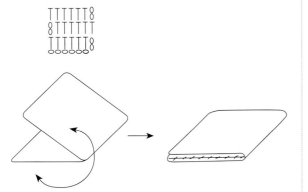

Fold in half lengthways and stitch the selvedge edges together.

Making up

Attach the toy safety eyes. Using the photographs as reference and matching yarn, fill the head and body with toy stuffing, and attach the head to the body. Stitch the ears, eyes, and beak to the face and the hat between the ears. Finally, stitch the tummy to the body and make it look like the clever little owl it is!

Cute Little Baby

When the stork brings that special bundle of joy, it's time to welcome the new arrival with pretty little presents. So why not make the bouncing baby his or her very own mini-me?

Size

Height: 4 in. (10 cm)

Materials

HOOK SIZE: C (3 mm)

YARN:

Flesh-colored for the head

White for the pacifier and bib

Dark pink for the body and bib

Light pink for the cheeks

Yellow for the hair

OTHER MATERIALS:

Toy stuffing

Black beads, .16 in. (4 mm)

Head

Using flesh-colored yarn, make a magic ring as follows.

Make a loop with tail end of yarn on right, keeping ball end on left. Pull the ball end through loop. Make one chain through loop on hook you have drawn through to steady the circle. Work 6 sc into the circle and complete with sl st into the first sc. See also page 13.

1st round: 2 sc into each sc. (12 sts)

2nd round: [1 sc into next sc, 2 sc into foll 1 sc] 6 times. (18 sts)

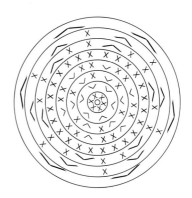

4th–7th rounds

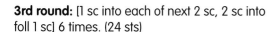

3rd round: [1 sc into each of next 2 sc, 2 sc into foll 1 sc] 6 times. (24 sts)

4th–7th rounds: 1 sc into each sc.

8th round: [1 sc into each of next 2 sc, sc 2 tog] 6 times. (18 sts)

Fill the head with toy stuffing.

9th round: [1 sc into next sc, sc 2 tog] 6 times. (12 sts)

10th round: [sc 2 tog] 6 times. (6 sts)

Fasten off.

Body

Using dark pink yarn, make a magic ring as for the head.

1st round: 2 sc into each sc. (12 sts)

2nd round: [1 sc into next sc, 2 sc into foll sc] 6 times. (18 sts)

3rd round: 1 sc into each sc.

Repeat the last round until the piece measures 1.2 in. (3 cm).

Fasten off.

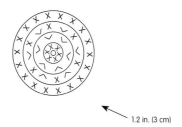

1.2 in. (3 cm)

Legs (make 2)

Using dark pink yarn, make a magic ring as for the head.

1st round: 1 sc into each sc. (6 sts)

Repeat the last round until the piece measures 1.2 in. (3 cm).

Fasten off.

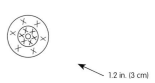

1.2 in. (3 cm)

Arms (make 2)

Using dark pink yarn, make a magic ring as for the head.

1st round: 1 sc into each sc. (6 sts)

Repeat the last round until the piece measures .8 in. (2 cm).

Fasten off.

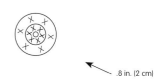

.8 in. (2 cm)

Bib

Using white yarn, make a magic ring as for the head.

1st round: 2 sc into each sc. (12 sts)

Fasten off white yarn. Join in dark pink yarn to any sc.

2nd round: 1 ch, 1 sc into sc at base of ch, [2 sc into the next sc, 1 sc into foll sc] 4 times.

Fasten off.

Cheeks (make 2)

Using light pink yarn, make a magic ring as for the head.

Fasten off.

Pacifier

Using white yarn, make a magic ring as for the head.

1st round: 1 sc into each sc. (6 sts)

Fasten off.

Making up

Using the photographs as reference and matching yarn, stitch the cheeks, pacifier and the black beads for the eyes in place. Using yellow yarn, embroider a chain stitch curl on to the head to represent hair. Stitch the head, arms, legs and bib to the body and a new amigurumi child is born!

What a Winner!

At moments of personal triumph, who doesn't want to feel like a complete winner? Let someone know that he or she is really special—whatever the event—with his or her very own gold medal and trophy.

Gold Trophy

Size

Height: 6.3 in. (16 cm)

Materials

HOOK SIZE: C (3 mm)

YARN:

Yellow for the main trophy sections

Dark yellow for the decoration

OTHER MATERIALS:

Toy stuffing

Cardboard

Structure

The gold trophy is worked in five sections.

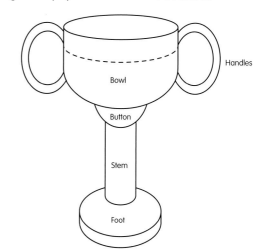

Bowl

Using yellow yarn, make a magic ring as follows.

Make a loop with tail end of yarn on right, keeping ball end on left. Pull the ball end through loop. Make one chain through loop on hook you have drawn through to steady the circle. Work 6 sc into the circle and complete with sl st into the first sc. See also page 13.

1st round: 2 sc into each sc. (12 sts)

2nd round: [1 sc into next sc, 2 sc into foll 1 sc] 6 times. (18 sts)

3rd round: [1 sc into each of next 2 sc, 2 sc into foll 1 sc] 6 times. (24 sts)

4th round: [1 sc into each of next 3 sc, 2 sc into foll 1 sc] 6 times. (30 sts)

5th round: [1 sc into each of next 4 sc, 2 sc into foll 1 sc] 6 times. (36 sts)

6th round: 1 sc into each sc.

7th round: [1 sc into each of next 5 sc, 2 sc into foll 1 sc] 6 times. (42 sts)

8th round: 1 sc into each sc.

9th round: [1 sc into each of next 6 sc, 2 sc into foll 1 sc] 6 times. (48 sts)

10th–23rd rounds: 1 sc into each sc.

Fasten off.

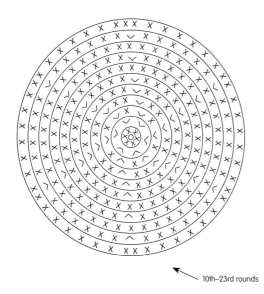

10th–23rd rounds

Button

Using yellow yarn, make a magic ring as for the bowl.

1st round: 2 sc into each sc. (12 sts)

2nd round: [1 sc into next sc, 2 sc into foll sc] 6 times. (18 sts)

3rd round: [1 sc into next 2 sc, 2 sc into foll sc] 6 times. (24 sts)

4th–7th rounds: 1 sc into each sc.

Fasten off.

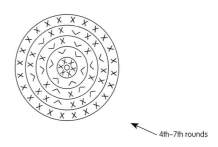

4th–7th rounds

Stem

Using yellow yarn, make a magic ring as for the bowl.

1st round: 2 sc into each sc. (12 sts)

2nd round: [1 sc into next sc, 2 sc into foll sc] 6 times. (18 sts)

3rd round: 1 sc into each sc.

Repeat the last round until the work measures 4 in. (10 cm).

Fasten off.

4 in. (10 cm)

Foot

Using yellow yarn, make a magic ring as for the bowl.

1st round: 2 sc into each sc. (12 sts)

2nd round: [1 sc into next sc, 2 sc into foll sc] 6 times. (18 sts)

3rd round: [1 sc into each of next 2 sc, 2 sc into foll sc] 6 times. (24 sts)

4th round: [1 sc into each of next 3 sc, 2 sc into foll sc] 6 times. (30 sts)

Measure and cut out a circle of cardboard to match the diameter of the work.

5th round: [1 sc into each of next 3 sc, sc 2 tog] 6 times. (24 sts)

6th round: [1 sc into each of next 2 sc, sc 2 tog] 6 times. (18 sts)

7th round: [1 sc into next sc, sc 2 tog] 6 times. (12 sts)

8th round: [sc 2 tog] 6 times. (6 sts)

Fasten off.

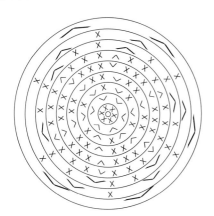

Handle (make 2)

Using yellow yarn, make a magic ring as for the bowl.

1st round: 2 sc into each sc. (12 sts)

2nd round: [1 sc into next sc, 2 sc into foll sc] 6 times. (18 sts)

3rd round: 1 sc into each sc.

Repeat the last row until the work measures 7 in. (18 cm) or the length required.

Fasten off.

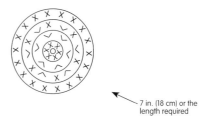

7 in. (18 cm) or the length required

Leaf decoration (make 2)

4 dc-bobble = [wrap the yarn around the hook, insert the hook into fourth ch from hook, wrap yarn around hook, draw yarn through ch, wrap yarn around hook, draw yarn through two loops on hook] 4 times, wrap yarn around hook, draw yarn through all loops on the hook.

Using dark yellow yarn, make 4 ch

1st row: 4 dc-bobble [4 ch, 4 dc-bobble] 13 times or as many times as you wish to twist around the handle.

Fasten off.

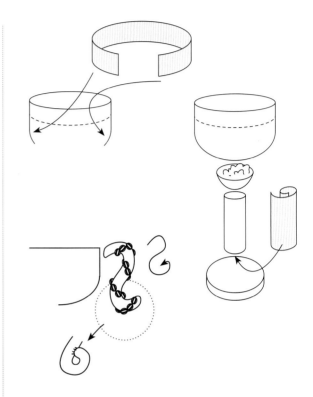

Making up

Cut the cardboard to match the length of the stem and roll it into a cylinder shape. Insert the cardboard roll and toy stuffing into the stem.

Cut the cardboard 1.2 in. (3 cm) deep to match the circumference of the bowl and twist it into a ring shape. Insert the ring into the bowl and fold the top edge over to cover the cardboard. Stitch in place.

Fill the button and lightly fill the handles with toy stuffing.

Using the photographs as reference and matching yarn, attach the foot to the stem, the stem to the button, and the button to the bowl. Then, stitch the top of each handle to the lip of the bowl, and shape and stitch the lower handle in place. Arrange the lengths of leaf decoration and stitch in place. What a winner!

Gold medal

Size

Disc width: 3.5 in. (9 cm)

Materials

HOOK SIZE: C (3 mm)

YARN:

Yellow for the medal

Dark yellow for the medal decoration

Blue, white, and red for the ribbon

OTHER MATERIALS:

Toy stuffing

Medal (make 2)

Using yellow yarn, make a magic ring as follows.

Make a loop with tail end of yarn on right, keeping ball end on left. Pull the ball end through loop. Make one chain through loop on hook you have drawn through to steady the circle. Work 6 sc into the circle and complete with sl st into the first sc. See also page 13.

1st round: 2 sc into each sc. (12sts)

2nd round: [1 sc into next sc, 2 sc into foll 1 sc] 6 times. (18 sts)

3rd round: [1 sc into each of next 2 sc, 2 sc into foll 1 sc] 6 times. (24 sts)

4th round: [1 sc into each of next 3 sc, 2 sc into foll sc] 6 times. (30 sts)

5th round: [1 sc into each of next 4 sc, 2 sc into foll sc] 6 times. (36 sts)

6th–7th rounds: 1 sc into each sc.

Fasten off.

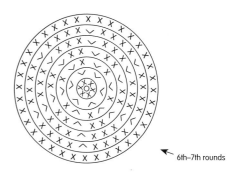

6th–7th rounds

Leafy decoration (make 2)

Using dark yellow yarn, make 26 ch.

1st row: sl st into the fifth ch from the hook, sl st into next ch, [5 ch, sl st into base of 5 ch, sl st into next ch] 10 times.

Do not work the remaining ch.

Fasten off.

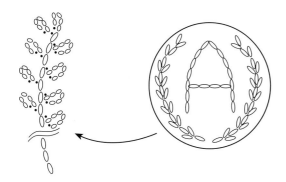

Letter or motif

Draw a life size cartoon of the letter or motif and divide into sections that can be crocheted.

Using dark yellow yarn, make a ch long enough for the first section of the letter

1st row: 1 sc into the second ch from the hook, 1 sc into each ch to end.

Fasten off.

Repeat for each section of the letter or motif.

For curves, work two double crochet stitches into the same stitch as required.

Ribbon

Using red yarn, make a ch long enough to fit around the neck.

1st row: 1 hdc into the third ch from the hook, 1 hdc into each ch to end.

Fasten off red yarn, and join in white yarn.

2nd row: 2 ch, 1 hdc into each hdc.

Fasten off white yarn, and join in blue yarn.

3rd row: 2 ch, 1 hdc into each hdc.

Fasten off.

Making up

Place the two medal pieces on top of each other with your preferred side facing out. Using matching yarn, sew the two pieces together around most of the outer edge, fill with toy stuffing, and complete the seam.

Then, using the photographs as reference, attach the leaf decoration and any other motif you may have crocheted.

Using yellow yarn, join in to the top of the medal about .6 in. (1.5 cm) to the right of the center top, make a ch long enough to reach a point about .6 in. (1.5 cm) to the right of the center top, and sl st through the seam stitches at this point. Turn, 1 ch, work sc sts around the ch, back along its length.

Fasten off.

Thread the crochet ribbon through the loop and stitch the ribbon ends together.

It's definitely a winner!

Happy New Home

Mark that special move into a home of one's own—be it baby bungalow or penthouse apartment—with a cute, crocheted cottage. Just remember, there's no place like home.

Size

Height: 8 in. (20 cm)

Materials

HOOK SIZE: C (3 mm)

YARN:

Light brown for the walls and base

Blue for the roof

White for the windows and doors

Brown for the window frames

Red for the doorframe

Yellow and turquoise for the tiles

Emerald green for the grass

Dark green for the grass

OTHER MATERIALS:

Toy stuffing

Cardboard

Structure

Start by cutting cardboard to support the house structure.

The size can vary; however, edges that meet must be the same length.

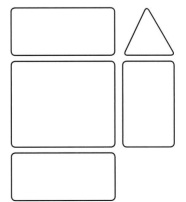

The house shown:

Roof (x1), 4 x 5.5 in. (10 x 14 cm): fold in half so each half is 4 x 2.7 in. (10 x 7 cm).

Walls (x1), 13.4 in. x 3.1 in. (34 x 8 cm): fold into four sections of 4 in. (10 cm) (front), 2.7 in. (7 cm) (side), 4 in. (10 cm) (back), 2.7 in. (7 cm) (side), along the length. Join the end edges with tape.

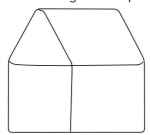

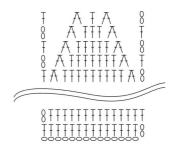

Sides (one of each)

Using light brown yarn, make a 16 ch or a ch as wide as the section of cardboard for the sides.

1st row: 1 hdc into the third ch from the hook, 1 hdc into each ch, turn.

2nd row: 2 ch (counts as first hdc), 1 hdc into the back loop of each sc, turn.

Repeat the last row until the piece measures 3.1 in. (8 cm) or matches the depth of the section of cardboard for the sides before the shaping.

Next row: 2 ch, (counts as first hdc), hdc 2 tog, hdc into each hdc until 3 sts rem, hdc 2 tog, 1 hdc into last top of beg ch, turn.

Repeat the last row until no sts remain and the selvedge measures 2.7 in. (7 cm) or matches the depth of the section of cardboard for the roof—if necessary work decrease sts in the center of the row.

Fasten off.

Front and Back (one of each)

Using light brown yarn, make a 21 ch or a ch as wide as the section of cardboard for the front and back.

1st row: 1 hdc into the third ch from the hook, 1 hdc into each ch, turn.

2nd row: 2 ch (counts as first hdc), 1 hdc into the back loop of each sc, turn.

Repeat the last row until the piece measures 3.1 in. (8 cm) or matches the depth of the section of cardboard for the front and back.

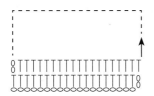

Base

Using light brown yarn, make a 16 ch or a ch as wide as the section of cardboard for the sides.

1st row: 1 hdc into the third ch from the hook, 1 hdc into each ch, turn.

2nd row: 2 ch (counts as first hdc), 1 hdc into the back loop of each sc, turn.

Repeat the last row until the piece measures 4 in. (10 cm) or matches the width of the section of cardboard for the front and back.

Roof (make 2)

Using blue yarn, make a 21 ch or a ch as wide as the section of cardboard for the roof.

1st row: 1 hdc into the third ch from the hook, 1 hdc into each ch, turn.

2nd row: 2 ch (counts as first hdc), 1 hdc into the back loop of each sc, turn.

Repeat the last row until the piece measures 2.7 in. (7 cm) or matches the depth of the section of cardboard for half the roof.

Fasten off.

Seam the two roof section together along the top edges of the last row.

Tiles

Using yellow yarn, join into the first line of exposed front loop of the roof section on the right edge.

1st row: [2 ch, skip 1 st, 5 dc into the next front loop, 2 ch, skip 1 st, 1 sc into next st] to end, ending with either a sc or 5 dc sts.

Fasten off yellow yarn, and join in turquoise yarn into the next line of front loops.

2nd row: 2 ch, 5 dc into base of ch, 2 ch, skip 1 st, 1 sc into next st, [2 ch, skip 1 st, 5 dc into the next front loop, 2 ch, skip 1 st, 1 sc into next st] repeat to end, ending with either a sc or 5 dc sts.

Fasten off green yarn, and join in orange yarn into the next line of front loops.

Repeat the last 2 rows until the desired number of front loops have been covered.

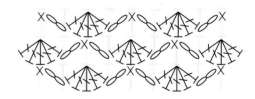

Larger grass section

Using emerald green yarn, make a magic ring as follows.

Make a loop with tail end of yarn on right, keeping ball end on left. Pull the ball end through loop. Make one chain through loop on hook you have drawn through to steady the circle. Work 6 sc into the circle and complete with sl st into the first sc. See also page 13.

1st round: 2 sc into each sc. (12 sts)

2nd round: [1 sc into next sc, 2 sc into foll 1 sc] 6 times. (18 sts)

3rd round: [1 sc into each of next 2 sc, 2 sc into foll 1 sc] 6 times. (24 sts)

4th round: [1 sc into each of next 3 sc, 2 sc into foll sc] 6 times. (30 sts)

5th round: [1 sc into each of next 4 sc, 2 sc into foll sc] 6 times. (36 sts)

6th round: [1 sc into each of next 5 sc, 2 sc into foll sc] 6 times. (42 sts)

7th round: [1 sc into each of next 6 sc, 2 sc into foll sc] 6 times. (48 sts)

8th round: [1 sc into each of next 7 sc, 2 sc into foll sc] 6 times. (54 sts)

9th round: [1 sc into each of next 8 sc, 2 sc into foll sc] 6 times. (60 sts)

Fasten off.

Smaller grass section

Using dark green yarn, make a magic ring as for the larger grass section.

Work as for the larger grass section until the 6th round has been completed.

Fasten off.

Front door

Using white yarn, make 7 ch.

1st row: 1 hdc into the third ch from the hook, 1 hdc into each ch, turn. (6 sts)

2nd–3rd rows: 2 ch (counts as first hdc), 1 hdc into the back loop of each sc, turn.

4th row: 2 ch, skip 1 hdc, hdc into the back loop of each of next 4 sc.

Fasten off.

Using red yarn, join into the lower right edge and work a round of sc sts around the door.

Window

Using white yarn, make a magic ring as for larger grass section.

1st round: 2 sc into each sc. (12 sts)

2nd round: [1 sc into next sc, 2 sc into foll sc] 6 times. (18 sts)

3rd round: [1 sc into each of next 2 sc, 2 sc into foll sc] 6 times. (24 sts)

4th round: [1 sc into each of next 3 sc, 2 sc into foll sc] 6 times. (30 sts)

Fasten off white yarn, and join in brown.

5th round: [1 sc into each of next 4 sc, 2 sc into foll sc] 6 times.

Fasten off.

Making up

Using the structure diagram and photographs as reference, stitch the front, back, side, and roof pieces. Place the cardboard inside the house against the sides and hold in place with toy stuffing. Stitch the base to the bottom of the house. Using red yarn and a French knot, embroider a doorknob onto the door. Using brown yarn and chain stitch, embroider window frames onto the door. Stitch the door and window in place. Stitch a short section of the two pieces of grass together. This is the house that you built!

Great Job!

Celebrate a step up the career ladder, and crochet up this crazy little computer with its very own mousey mouse when you want to say congratulations on landing that plum new job.

Size

Computer height: 3.3 in. (8.5 cm)

Mouse length: 2.2 in. (5.5 cm)

Materials

HOOK SIZE: C (3 mm)

YARN.

Gray for the screen and the mouse

White for the body

Yellow for the computer nose

Pink for the mouse nose

OTHER MATERIALS:

Toy stuffing

2 toy safety eyes, .32 in. (8 mm)

2 black beads, .16 in. (4 mm)

Structure

The computer is made up of a monitor and a base. The monitor is made up of three pieces: the screen, the back, and one sidepiece, which is wrapped around four sides of the computer—all these pieces are worked in half treble stitches. And then there is a mouse, which is a mouse!

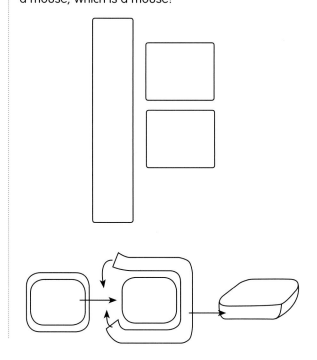

Computer screen

Using gray yarn, make 16 ch.

1st row: 1 hdc into the third ch from the hook, 1 hdc into each ch, turn. (15 sts)

2nd row: 2 ch, (counts as first hdc st), 1 hdc into each hdc, turn.

Repeat the last row 4 times more.

Fasten off.

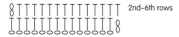

2nd–6th rows

Computer back

Using white yarn, make 16 ch.

Work as for computer screen.

Computer sides (make 2)

Using white yarn, make 6 ch.

1st row: 1 hdc into the third ch from the hook, 1 hdc into each ch, turn. (5 sts)

2nd row: 2 ch, (counts as first hdc st), 1 hdc into each hdc, turn.

Repeat the last row until the piece will fit around the edge of the screen and computer back.

Fasten off. The two pieces need to be seamed and stuffed.

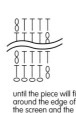

until the piece will fit around the edge of the screen and the computer back

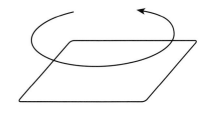

Computer base

Using white yarn, make 17 ch.

1st row: 1 sc into the second ch from the hook, 1 sc into each ch, turn. (16 sts)

2nd row: 1 ch, 1 sc into each sc, turn.

Repeat the last row 10 times more.

Fasten off.

2nd–12th rows

Computer nose

Using yellow yarn, make a magic ring as follows.

Make a loop with tail end of yarn on right, keeping ball end on left. Pull the ball end through loop. Make one chain through loop on hook you have drawn through to steady the circle. Work 6 sc into the circle and complete with sl st into the first sc. See also page 13.

1st–2nd rounds: 1 sc into each sc. (6 sts)

Fasten off.

1st–2nd rounds

Mouse

Using gray yarn, make a magic ring as for the computer nose.

1st round: 2 sc into each sc. (12 sts)

2nd–3rd rounds: 1 sc into each sc.

4th round: [1 sc into next sc, 2 sc into foll 1 sc] 6 times. (18 sts)

5th–9th rounds: 1 sc into each sc.

Fill the mouse with toy stuffing.

10th round: [1 sc into next sc, sc 2 tog] 6 times. (12 sts)

11th round: [sc 2 tog] 6 times. (6 sts)

Fasten off.

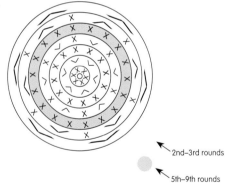

2nd–3rd rounds

5th–9th rounds

Mouse nose

Using pink yarn, make a magic ring as for the computer nose.

Fasten off.

Making up

Using the photographs as reference, attach the computer nose and toy safety eyes to the computer screen.

Pin the computer sides to the computer screen edge and, using matching yarn, stitch in place.

Pin the computer back to the computer sides and sew the two pieces together around most of the outer edge. Fill with toy stuffing and complete the seam.

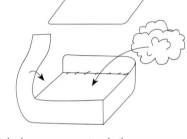

To finish the mouse: attach the mouse nose to the mouse; make ears by embroidering large loops on to the head; add whiskers by stitching through the nose, making a small anchoring stitch, cutting the yarn and leaving the ends free, repeat once more; stitch the black beads in place for eyes.

To connect your mouse to the computer, using gray yarn work a chain—there is no need for a USB cable!

Index

abbreviations, 9

amigurumi culture, 6-7

Angel Girl, 36, 37, 40, 41

anime, 7

arms, 28, 64-65, 89, 94, 122

baby, 120, 121, 122-123

ball shapes, 16

Big Heart Bear, 62, 63, 64-65

birds

    Ducks, 76, 77, 78-79

    Love Birds, 58, 59, 60-61

    owl, 114, 115, 116-118, 119

    Turkey, 46, 47, 48-49

Birthday Cake, 98, 99, 100-103

bow, 69, 71

bow tie, 71

boxes, 96-97

bride, 66, 67, 68-70

Candles, 42, 43, 44-45, 101-102, 103

chains, 10

    ring, 13

champagne bottle, 104, 105, 106-107

cherries, 102

Christmas Tree, 20, 21, 22-23, 29

computer, 138, 139, 140-141

computer mouse, 139, 141

crochet charts, reading, 9

crochet hooks, 8

    holding, 10

    sizes, 9

    suppliers, 144

Cute Little Baby, 120, 121, 122-123

Daffodils, 80, 81, 82, 83

designs, 15

disc shapes, 16

double crochet, 13

Dragon, 50, 51, 52-54, 55

Ducks, 76, 77, 78-79

ears, 34, 65, 89, 95, 117

Easter Bunny, 86, 87, 88-89

Eggs in Basket, 84, 85

ends, weaving in, 14

fastening off, 14

finishing off, 14

flames, 44, 102

gift boxes, 96-97

Gold medal, 125, 129-131

Gold Trophy, 124, 125, 126-128

Great Job!, 138, 139, 140-141

groom, 69-71

hair, 27, 40, 40, 68

half-double crochet, 13

Happy New Home, 132, 133, 134-137

Hooray Bubbles!, 104, 104, 105, 106-107

house, 132, 133, 134-137

kebab, 108, 109, 110-111

legs, 28, 33, 39, 53, 65, 70, 89, 94, 122

letters, 130

Love Birds, 58, 59, 60-61

magic ring, the, 11
   completing, 12
   making, 11-12
manga, 7
materials, 8
   choosing, 15
mohair, 8
motifs, 130
mouse, 139, 141

needles, 8
New Year Dragon, 50, 51, 52-54, 55

Oh So Clever!, 114, 115, 116-118, 119
owl, 114, 115, 116-118, 119

panda, 92, 93, 94-95
Party Animal, 92, 93, 94-95
patterns, reading, 9
pins, 8

rabbit, 86, 87, 88-89
rectangles, 17
Reindeer, 30, 31, 35
rhomboid shapes, 17
Rose, 72-73
round, working in the, 11-12

Santa Claus, 24, 25, 26-29
shapes, making, 16-17
single crochet, 13
sketching, 15
Special Gifts, 96-97
Springtime Ducks, 76, 77, 78-79

squares, 17
stars, 23
stitches
   chain, 10
   counting, 10
   double crochet, 13
   half-double crochet, 13
   slip, 10-11
   single crochet, 13
   stuffing, 8, 14, 54, 65, 71
   suppliers, 144
supports, 8, 45, 72, 82, 128, 137

teardrop shapes, 16
techniques, 10-13
teddy bear, 62, 63, 64-65
Thanksgiving Turkey, 46, 47, 48-49
thread, 8
Time to Party!, 108, 109, 110-111
tools, 8

Turkey, 46, 47, 48-49

wadding, 8
websites, 144
Wedding Joy, 66, 67, 68-71
What a Winner!
   Gold medal, 125, 129-131, 131
   Gold Trophy, 124, 125, 126-128, 128
wings, 61, 79

yarn, 8
holding, 10
suppliers, 144

Resources

Enter the Happy Cute world of amigurumi. The following tried-and-tested retailers and suppliers can help you on your mission to fill your life with cuteness.

Yarns

Blue Sky Alpacas, Inc.
P.O. Box 88
Cedar, MN 55011
www.blueskyalpacas.com

Brown Sheep Yarn Company
10062 County Road
Mitchell, NE 69357
www.brownsheep.com

Knitting Fever, Inc.
www.knittingfever.com

Knitty City
208 W. 79th St.
New York, NY 10024
www.knittycity.com

Lion Brand Yarns
135 Kero Road
Carlstadt, NJ 07072
www.lionbrand.com

Misti Alpaca
P.O.Box 2532
Glen Ellyn, Illinois 60138
www.mistialpaca.com

Patons
320 Livingstone Avenue South
Listowel, ON N4W 3H3
www.patonsyarns.com

Hooks

Clover
www.clover-usa.com

Herrschners
www.herrschners.com

Useful Information

If you are stuck for an idea or missing tools and materials, there is a serious online community support network of crochet and amigurumi enthusiasts. Check out *The Crochet Guild of America* (*www.crochet.org*) for crochet news, links to resources, and tips and advice. Try *Etsy* (*www.etsy.com*) for patterns, accessories, books, and all your other amigurumi needs.